Live Christ!
Give Christ!

Prayers for the New Evangelization

Compiled by Margaret Kerry, FSP

Introductions by Mary Lea Hill, FSP
With a Foreword by Archbishop Rino Fisichella

Pauline
BOOKS & MEDIA
Boston

Nihil Obstat: Reverend Thomas W. Buckley, S.T.D., S.S.L.

Imprimatur: ✠ Seán Cardinal O'Malley, O.F.M. Cap.
Archbishop of Boston
October 7, 2014

Cover design by Rosana Usselmann

Cover art by Ann Chapin

ISBN 10: 0-8198-4576-0

ISBN 13: 978-0-8198-4576-4

Published by Pauline Books & Media, 50 Saint Pauls Avenue, Boston, MA 02130-3491

Printed in the U.S.A.

www.pauline.org

Pauline Books & Media is the publishing house of the Daughters of St. Paul, an international congregation of women religious serving the Church with the communications media.

1 2 3 4 5 6 7 8 9   20 19 18 17 16 15

*Address of Pope Francis
to the Pauline Family*

Dear Brothers and Sisters of the Pauline Family!

I encourage you to continue on the path that Father Alberione began and that your Family has taken until now, keeping your gaze always fixed on vast horizons. This [evangelizing] impetus is toward "peoples" but also to the existential peripheries, a "Catholic" impetus. You all have this in your blood, in your DNA, for the very reason that your Founder was inspired by the person and the mission of the Apostle Paul.

In proclaiming Jesus and the Gospel to the masses, Blessed James Alberione saw the most authentic and necessary love that one can offer to men and women thirsty for truth and justice. He was deeply touched by the words of Saint Paul: "Woe to me if I do not preach the Gospel!" (1 Cor 9:16) and made them the ideal of his own life and mission. In following the footsteps of Jesus and imitating the Apostle of the Gentiles, he understood how to see the crowds as stray sheep, in need of sure directions for the journey of life. He thus spent his entire existence breaking the bread of the Word with them, using language suited to the times. In this way, you too are called to serve, with creativity and dynamic faithfulness to your charism, the people of today, whom the Spirit sends to you, identifying the most appropriate ways, in order that Jesus may be proclaimed. The vast horizons of evangelization and the urgent need to bear witness to the Gospel: don't just speak the words. Bear witness to it with your life. This testimony to all is the field of your apostolate. Many are still waiting to meet Jesus Christ. The vision of charity knows no limits and knows how to open ever new avenues to bring the breath of the Gospel into cultures and to the most diverse areas of society. . . .

Dear brothers and sisters, may the Holy Virgin, Mother of the Church, protect you, aid you, and be a sure guide on the path of the Pauline Family, in order that you may bring to fruition every initiative for good.

Contents

Foreword . . . . *xiii*

Introduction *1*

Prayers to the Most Holy Trinity *9*

Consecration to the Most Holy Trinity *11*

Praise to You, Holy Trinity *12*

Called to Communion *13*

Prayer of Trust *14*

Prayer to the Spirit for
Transformation in Christ *14*

Praise and Thanksgiving
for the Gifts of the Spirit *15*

Invocations to the Holy Spirit *16*

To Love as You Love *18*

I Believe *19*

My Vocation Prayer *20*

PRAYERS TO JESUS, WAY, TRUTH, AND LIFE *21*

Our Secret of Success *23*

God's Dream for Me *24*

"I Am with You" *25*

Invocations to Jesus Master *26*

You in Me *27*

To Jesus, Our Master and Teacher *27*

Lord, You Are My All *28*

Kenosis in Jesus *29*

Live in Us, Jesus *30*

Draw Us to You *31*

May I Be in You *31*

Chosen and Loved in Christ Jesus *32*

We Adore You Living in the Church *33*

PRAYERS TO MARY, QUEEN OF THE APOSTLES *35*

Consenting to the Word *37*

A Prayer to Say *Yes* Like Mary *37*

O Mary, Make Me an Apostle *38*

Mary, Woman of Communication *39*

Receive Me, O Mary *40*

Mary, Transformer of the Apostles *41*

Prayer to Mary for Families *42*

Prayer to Mary for a Listening Heart *43*

To Our Lady of the Annunciation *44*

Queen of Apostles, Pray for Us! *45*

PRAYING WITH SAINT PAUL *47*

Saint Paul, Intercede for Us *49*

My Damascus Event *49*

I Know the One in Whom I Put My Trust *51*

Love Never Fails *53*

Paul's Prayer to Our Triune God *54*

Teach Us to Live in Intimacy with Christ *55*

Recall Saint Paul's Example *55*

Lead Us, Apostle Paul *56*

Prayer for Patience *56*

Love Builds Up *57*

Paul's Prayer for Transformation in Christ *58*

To Know That I Am Loved *59*

Prayers for Those Engaged
in the New Evangelization 61

Prayer for Discipleship 63

Living the Gospel 64

For the Church's Mission of Evangelization 64

Who Will Lead Others to God? 65

Prayer for Apostolic Discernment 65

Jesus, Good Shepherd 66

The Evangelizer's Power Idea 66

Sent by the Spirit 67

Prayer to Witness to the Gospel 68

Opening Our Hearts to the World 68

An Evangelizer's Prayer 69

Praying the Beatitudes 70

Prayer for Openness of Heart 71

Prayer to Incarnate Christ in Our Culture 71

May We Be Instruments of Justice and Peace 72

New Peace Prayer of Saint Francis 73

The World Is Waiting 74

Prayer for Evangelization 74

For Those Who Do Not Know God 75

Creed of Those Called to Evangelize 75

Evangelization Prayer for One
    Who Is Elderly or Infirm 77

A Catechist's Prayer 77

A Youth Minister's Prayer 78

To Radiate God 78

How Beautiful to Communicate Jesus 79

Prayer to Be Trustworthy Companions 79

EVANGELIZING IN A COMMUNICATIONS CULTURE . . . 81

A Eucharistic Offertory for the Media
    (Pauline Offertory) 84

Prayer for Using the Media
    in the New Evangelization 86

Canticle of Praise for the Media 87

Prayer to Saint Paul for the Media:
    A New Place of Evangelization 88

Prayer for True Communication 90

A Communicator's Prayer 90

Prayer for Creativity in the Work
    of Evangelizing 91

To Jesus, Master of Images 92

Help Us Be Discerning Users of the Media 93

A Photographer's Prayer 93

A Graphic Designer's Prayer *94*

An Artist's Prayer *95*

Proclaiming Christ through the Media Arts *96*

A Musician's Prayer *97*

Make Me Life for the World *97*

Prayer for Good Use of the Media *99*

To Saint Gabriel the Archangel, Patron of
   the Electronic and Digital Media *100*

A Prayer Before Writing *101*

A Storyteller's Prayer *102*

Praying the News *103*

The Word of God *105*

Speak Through Us, Lord *107*

At Home with the Word *107*

A Heart Open to Your Word *108*

Treasures of Your Word *108*

Before Reading Sacred Scripture *109*

After Reading Sacred Scripture *110*

Prayer of an Apostle of the Word *111*

To Be Your Living Word *112*

Becoming Bread Broken for the World *112*

Jesus, Word of the Father *113*

Prayer to Mary for the Ministers of the Word . . . *114*

THE HOLY EUCHARIST *115*

A Visit with Jesus *117*

Prayer to Begin Eucharistic Adoration *118*

Dwell in My Heart, Lord *118*

To Jesus, Our Eucharistic Master *119*

Act of Trust in the Promises of Jesus *120*

The Eucharist: Bread of the Strong *121*

The Eucharist: Bread of the Covenant *122*

May My Life Be a Liturgy *123*

Emmaus Prayer *123*

Prayer of the Disciple of the Eucharistic Master . . . *124*

My Beloved Jesus *125*

Bread of Wisdom *126*

PRAYERS OF RECONCILIATION AND FORGIVENESS . . . *129*

Prayer Before an Examination of Conscience *133*

Prayer After an Examination of Conscience *133*

May I See Myself as You See Me *134*

To Jesus, the Divine Healer *134*

For Unfailing Hope *135*

Prayer to Grow in Love *136*

To Live and Communicate Peace *137*

Spiritual Healing Prayer *138*

Wonders of Mercy *139*

LIST OF CONTRIBUTORS *141*

Foreword

The path of the New Evangelization entails the recovery of a healthful spirituality—a real condition that would enable people to return to their interior lives while transcending the noise, tumult, and contradictions that they face on a daily basis. Thus, the words of Saint Augustine are as true today as they ever were, for they remind us of the importance of contemplation that leads us naturally to silence, listening, and prayer: "Do not go outside yourself but return to within yourself; truth dwells in the inner man; and if you find that your nature is changeable, transcend yourself" (*De vera religione* 39, 72).

The primacy of contemplation in the mission of the New Evangelization continues to be a central theme in both the teaching and preaching of Pope Francis: "What is needed is the ability to cultivate an interior space which can give a Christian meaning to commitment and activity. Without prolonged moments of adoration, of prayerful encounter with the word, of sincere conversation with the Lord, our work easily becomes meaningless . . . and our fervor dies out" (Pope Francis, *Apostolic Exhortation Evangelii Gaudium*, no. 262). Therefore, in order not to "run in vain" (Gal 2:2) on the road of evangelization, we need to focus on contemplation, which is most essential in order to keep our eyes ever fixed on the face of Christ. For the "first proclamation" that every Christian is called upon to undertake is to live in Christ in order to know how to share him with others.

The following work, *Live Christ! Give Christ! Prayers for the New Evangelization*, contains prayers written by Blessed James Alberione and other contemporary Paulines. Such a valuable work will be of great assistance to modern men and women who are often deafened to the Divine because of the cacophonies of atheism, agnosticism, secularism, and relativism, and, thus, are thwarted in their intent to live lives that possess a deeper meaning. Further, the beauty and cogency of these prayers will serve to place each individual into a more profound silence before God, which, ultimately, will lead to a uniquely personal encounter with Jesus Christ. The special graces received by means of contemplation and prayer will inspire within each person a greater capacity to know how to give an explanation of his or her own faith, showing forth Jesus Christ, the Son of God, the sole Savior of the human race. To the extent that we are capable of this, we will be able to offer our contemporaries the response they are awaiting. The new evangelization begins from this point, from the conviction that grace acts upon us and transforms us to the point of bringing about a conversion of heart, and of the credibility of our witness.

Archbishop Rino Fisichella

President of the Pontifical Council for the Promotion of the New Evangelization

Introduction

One of the most beautiful treasures of the Catholic Church is the number and variety of spiritualities that have arisen within the great religious families. Among the best known are the Benedictine, Franciscan, Dominican, Ignatian, and Carmelite spiritualities. There are, of course, many others, each presenting its followers with a particular way of praying. For example, the Franciscans center their spirituality around the poor Christ, stressing the virtues of humility and simplicity, while the spirituality of the Benedictines is centered on Sacred Scripture and the liturgy.

From the earliest times of Christianity until today, new spiritual traditions have come into being according to the needs of a particular era of history. In the early twentieth century, God inspired a young priest from northern Italy to develop a spirituality that would meet the needs and challenges of the Church charged with the mandate to evangelize in the age of communication.

On the night bridging the nineteenth and twentieth centuries, a sixteen-year-old seminarian named James Alberione was immersed in Eucharistic adoration in the Cathedral of Alba. He had taken to heart Pope Leo XIII's recent appeal that the Church ready herself to engage the dawning of a new world of ideologies and inventions, the likes of which had never been seen before. In his earnest prayer that evening, Alberione mulled over the pope's challenge and, before the night was over, felt entrusted with a particular vision for the new century. In time, his inspiration would give birth to the Pauline Family, which would be composed of ten foundations, both religious and lay. The religious Congregations include:

- The Society of St. Paul (founded in 1914), priests and brothers who spread the Gospel using the modern means of communication.

- The Daughters of St. Paul (1915), sisters with an identical mission to that of the Society of St. Paul.

- The Sister Disciples of the Divine Master (1924), who devote themselves to the liturgical apostolate.
- The Sisters of the Good Shepherd (1938), who carry out the pastoral apostolate.
- The Sisters of the Queen of Apostles (1959), who work for the formation and recruitment of vocations within the Church.

In addition to these, Alberione founded four Lay Institutes in 1960, whose members would bring his vision into every corner of life. They include:

- The Institute of Jesus the Priest for secular priests;
- The Institute of Mary of the Annunciation for single women;
- The Institute of St. Gabriel the Archangel for single men;
- The Holy Family Institute for married couples.

Father Alberione also invited lay collaborators to work with him from the very beginning of the Pauline Family. He relied upon certain generous lay men and women for help in evangelization as well as for prayerful and financial support. In 1918 he organized this group into the Association of Pauline Cooperators, men and women who recognize the call to share in the spirit and mission of the Pauline Family and who, after a brief period of formation, make formal promises as part of their association.

Together these religious and lay Paulines would adopt their founder's vision and make it a living, breathing reality in the Church. One hundred years later, under the inspiration of now-Blessed James Alberione, his sons and daughters around the world continue to channel their spiritual and apostolic energies into the proclamation of the Gospel of Jesus Christ using all the means available in our digital age.

Key to Blessed James Alberione's success was his ability to integrate spirit and life. Not only did he empower those who followed him to evangelize with the means of communication (beginning with the "good press," as he called it, and then "any other means offered by technical progress"), he also under-girded this with an intense prayer life that embraced the needs of humanity in the desires and intentions of the media apostles.

In Alberione's spirituality, communication with God through prayer enlivens communication with men and women, and efforts to open the channels of grace always take into account the necessity to make reparation for evil—especially evil done because of the misuse of the media. Alberione's goal was the basic Gospel call: "Glory to God and peace to humanity." He centered his spirituality in Scripture and the Eucharist. To the whole Pauline Family he declared: "You were born of the Eucharist. Your food is the Eucharist. Your spirituality is the Gospel lived in its entirety, as explained by Saint Paul. Your Mother and model is Mary."

It is interesting to note that in developing a spirituality for these new apostles, Alberione purposefully drew on the earliest devotions of the Church. He re-introduced Jesus as the Divine Master or Teacher, Mary as the Queen of Apostles, and Saint Paul as the model Apostle, since he was the greatest evangelizer of the early Church. Pauline spirituality would develop around these three principal figures.

The one thing that all great spiritualities have in common is an emphasis on what the Church today calls the new evangelization. By this is meant the effort to redirect our lives toward Jesus and his saving message and to make the Gospel known and embraced by everyone. Pauline spirituality aims at conforming one's entire person to Christ, so that, rooted in him, one grows in holiness and becomes with him way, truth, and life for the world. The title of this book, which is taken from a directive Blessed Alberione issued to his followers, aptly sums up this process. Paulines are to "live Christ"—that is, to allow Christ the Master, Way, Truth, and Life, to live fully in them—so that they can then "give Christ" to the whole world. This is a spirituality for evangelizers of every age.

In the following pages readers will find prayers written by or based on the words of Blessed James Alberione, whom Pope John Paul II once called "the first apostle of the new evangelization." In addition there are prayers arising from the hearts of Paulines living today. Alberione encouraged the men and women who came after him to revitalize the Pauline charism with new works and new prayers, so that the great ongoing communication between God and his people would continue; that all of us would be inspired and strengthened in our call to transform the world, to build God's Kingdom for everyone; and that we would find the harmony of spirit and life of which Saint Paul spoke when he said, "It is no longer I who live, but it is Christ who lives in me" (Gal 2:20).

In Pope Francis' apostolic exhortation *Evangelii Gaudium*, he invited all Catholics to a renewed personal encounter with Jesus Christ, who calls us to share with all our sisters and brothers the joy of his Gospel. Each one of us, by virtue of our baptism, has been chosen and is sent by God to witness to others the incomparable gift of life in Christ Jesus. We carry out the mission of the Church each and every day by living and sharing our faith—in whatever occupation or state of life the Lord has called us to—not only with our words and actions, but especially through our prayer. Prayer is what roots us in God and keeps us in constant relationship with him. Prayer is what unites our hearts with Christ's heart, full of mercy and love for all people.

And so we offer this collection of prayers to you as a valuable means to deepen your relationship with our living God and to inspire you in accepting his invitation to announce the Gospel in our world today. May the Holy Spirit enlighten your mind, strengthen your will, and fill your heart with love as you proclaim the Gospel of Jesus Christ with your life and words, by your prayer and actions, in your home and workplace, to everyone you meet, whether in person or through social media.

Prayers to the
Most Holy Trinity

Our faith is founded on mystery. We believe in a God we cannot fully understand but can completely love. During his life among us, Jesus Christ revealed that God is one Being, but also a Trinity of Persons: a Father who loves his only-begotten Son from all eternity, sending him as his Word to our world; and the Holy Spirit who is the loving bond between them. God is love, and this is how he makes himself known to us. We were baptized in the name of the Father, Son, and Holy Spirit, becoming children of our mysterious God. Our Baptism freed us from the original sin that had separated humankind from God. We were filled with God's life and love; in fact, God lives within us as Saint Paul reminds us: "In him we live and move and have our being" (Acts 17:28).

Since we are created in the image of God, the Trinity's communication of love is the model for our communication and relationship with our brothers and sisters. In accepting God's gift of love, and loving him in return with his self-same gift, we come to desire and actively promote the good of others by leading them to God, the greatest good.

Our awesome God is Creator and Sustainer, Redeemer and Model, and Inspirer and Sanctifier. Although we profess our belief in the Triune God whenever we say the Creed, praise the Blessed Trinity whenever we pray the Gloria, and renew our Baptism whenever we sign ourselves with the Sign of the Cross, there are endless opportunities to speak to God—Father, Son, and Holy Spirit—in prayer.

Consecration to the Most Holy Trinity

O Divine Trinity,
Father, Son, and Holy Spirit,
present and active in the Church
and in the depths of my soul,
I adore you, I thank you, I love you!
And through the hands of Mary most holy,
I give myself entirely to you for life and for
    eternity.
To you, heavenly Father, I offer and give myself
    to be consecrated as your child.
To you, Jesus Master, I offer and give myself
    to be consecrated as your brother/sister and
    disciple.
To you, Holy Spirit, I offer and give myself to be
    consecrated as a "living temple" to be blessed
    and sanctified.
O Mary, Mother of the Church and my Mother,
teach me to live, through the liturgy and the
    sacraments,
in ever more intimate union with the three
    divine Persons,
so that my whole life may be a *glory to the Father,*
to the Son, and to the Holy Spirit. Amen.

Blessed James Alberione

Praise to You, Holy Trinity

God and Father of our Lord Jesus Christ;
Jesus Lord, Master and Shepherd;
Spirit of truth and love; Holy Trinity,
I thank you for the graces and blessings
    of this day—
those that I am aware of and the many more
    I have not recognized.

I ask forgiveness for my sins and failings.
Help me to become aware of offenses I may have
    given,
to ask pardon, and to forgive from the heart
anyone against whom I might have a grievance.

Bless everyone dear to me
and all those in need throughout the world.
Grant that each person now living
may persevere in your love until death.

Be with all who suffer.
Sustain them in their trials,
and in their final hour call them to yourself.

Be with me this night,
Father with a mother's heart,
Master with a shepherd's heart,
Spirit of life and love.

Should this night be my last,
I beg you to receive me into your presence—
not through any merit of mine,
but because of your mercy,
which is beyond anything I can ever imagine.
   Amen.

Called to Communion

Communion with you, triune God, allows me to be a fountain of living water filled to overflowing with your love. You make me a sharer in your divine communion and lead me to communion with others.

Yet, in this age of instantaneous communication, I often feel isolated in this midst of so much information, in the promise of relationships without effort, or in the distance between me and those in need.

Heal the fragmentation of my mind, will, and heart. Center me in you, my Father; in you, Jesus, Faithful One; in you, Spirit, who makes us whole and holy.

You know my name—I who am made in your image and likeness—you know me through and through. Allow me to be a reflection of you as I encounter others today, whether in person, over the phone, through social media, by e-mail, or in prayer.

Prayer of Trust

You, O my God, are always thinking of me. You are within me . . . around me. . . . My name is written on the palm of your hand. May I always and in all things do your will.

Lord, I abandon myself in you and relinquish all worry. I abandon myself completely in you, always.

My God, I want to be hidden in you, to lose myself in you like a drop of water in the ocean.

Venerable Thecla Merlo, FSP

Prayer to the Spirit for Transformation in Christ

Divine Holy Spirit, in a profound spirit of
    adoration
I ask that you unite my heart, my will, and my
    mind with those of Jesus.
May the affections of Jesus be my affections.
May the desires of Jesus be my desires.

May the thoughts of Jesus be my thoughts.

May Jesus himself live in my heart, my will,
and my mind.

I give Jesus my heart, so that he may be the one
who loves others in me and with me.

I give Jesus my will, so that he may be the one
who lives in me and with me.

I give Jesus my mind, so that he may be the one
who thinks in me and with me.

I want what he wants.

In me may he love.

In me may he decide.

In me may he act.

And may it be he himself who fulfills his mission through me.

Blessed James Alberione

Praise and Thanksgiving
for the Gifts of the Spirit

Jesus, my Master and Lord, I offer you praise and thanksgiving for your Spirit's presence within me.

At the moment of my Baptism, I became a new creation as God's adopted child; a temple and dwelling place of the Spirit. May I live each day in the

Spirit's presence, listening attentively for the Spirit's voice as I am gently led forward.

May my life overflow with the fruits of the Spirit's presence, reflecting love, joy, peace, patience, goodness, and faithfulness to all whom I meet.

I praise and thank you, Jesus, my Master and Lord, for your Spirit's presence within me.

Invocations to the Holy Spirit

Come, Holy Spirit, teach us to read and interpret the signs of the times.

Come, Holy Spirit, show us the seeds of truth present in the world.

Come, Holy Spirit, help us distinguish true prophets from false ones.

Come, Holy Spirit, develop in us that new person in Christ.

Come, Holy Spirit, reveal to us the secrets of God and the secrets of humanity.

Come, Holy Spirit, open our eyes that we may see you in all creation.

Come, Holy Spirit, deepen our awareness that God is love.

Come, Holy Spirit, set free in us the light and power of the word.

Come, Holy Spirit, pray the word in us.

Come, Holy Spirit, contemplate the word in us.

Come, Holy Spirit, adore the word in us.

Come, Holy Spirit, keep us in the word.

Come, Holy Spirit, comfort us with the word.

Come, Holy Spirit, celebrate in us the marvels of the word.

Come, Holy Spirit, infuse in us the spirit of docility to the word.

Come, Holy Spirit, sustain your Church, that we may be always faithful to your mission of salvation in the world.

Come, Holy Spirit, show every human person the urgent need to be reborn from on high.

Come, Holy Spirit, enable us to walk on the waters of the world with unshakable faith in the divine promise.

Come, Holy Spirit, illumine our minds.

Come, Holy Spirit, help us appreciate the gifts of life and of faith.

Come, Holy Spirit, remind us of everything Jesus has told us.

Come, Holy Spirit, teach us to live always in the presence of God.

Come, Holy Spirit, help us to share the Word with others.

To Love as You Love

Father, Just One, the world has not known you, but we have known you—imaged in Jesus, your Son—and we love you.

Help us make your name known to the ends of the earth, that all of us may live forever in you and you in us (see Jn 17:25–26), so that we may experience fullness of life.

Holy Spirit, as the Father and the Son pour themselves out completely in the dynamic of Trinitarian love, and as Jesus emptied himself in the incarnation and redemption to show us the way to the Father, enable us to pour ourselves out in faithful, loving service to our sisters and brothers. Sustain us in weariness and difficulties. Comfort us with your love.

Jesus, Master and Shepherd, Revealer and Lord, Servant and Savior, Living One, faithful and true, Amen of the Father, our new and living Way, ever interceding for us, help us to understand and live your call to faithful, loving service. Teach us to love as you love, to serve as you served, to be faithful as you are faithful. Amen.

I Believe

Father,
I believe in you;
I believe your revelation.

I believe that you call me
to live with you forever,
and that I owe this overwhelming gift
to the love of the Trinity for me,
expressed in the incarnation, life, death, and
    resurrection of Jesus, your Son,
and in the sending of the Holy Spirit.

I ask the Spirit to fill my heart
with love for you,
for Jesus, my Savior,
for the Spirit himself,
for Mary, my Mother,
and for all my sisters and brothers,
whose salvation Jesus has purchased
with his blood.

My Vocation Prayer

Heavenly Father,
grant me the grace to fulfill my calling
by following your way of incarnate love,
that I might make you known
to those I seek to serve in your name.
Let me imitate you, Jesus.
Let me take from the Church, the saints,
Scripture, theology, literature,
and share with others your food for the journey
so that they will come to you.
Let me absorb your life, Jesus.
Let me live in you so that others may live in you.
Holy Spirit, transform me; make me way, truth,
    and life
for my brothers and sisters.

Based on the writings of Blessed James Alberione

Prayers to Jesus, Way, Truth, and Life

The goal of the Pauline Family is to live Jesus Master, Way, Truth, and Life. It is how Jesus identifies himself in the Gospel: *"You call me Teacher and Lord—and you are right, for that is what I am"* (Jn 13:13). To his disciples he adds: *"I am the way, and the truth, and the life"* (Jn 14:6). Centering our life in Jesus as Master is more than a devotion; it embraces, permeates, and invigorates our whole person. Jesus wants us to look to him for everything, just as in ancient times students attached themselves to great teachers—absorbing their teachings, imitating their manner of living, and drawing strength from their company. As Christians called to live Christ and share Christ with others, we first must apprentice ourselves to him who is the Master of life.

Human beings are created in the image and likeness of God, and this is most profoundly evident in our faculties of mind, will, and heart (our abilities of reason, choice, and love). In our adherence to Jesus as Way, Truth, and Life, we imitate him, believe in him, live of his life of grace, and go forth as he did to proclaim to all people the Good News of salvation. *"I have set you an example, that you also should do as I have done to you"* (Jn 13:15).

Often our lives seem fragmented; we struggle to achieve balance and feel drawn in various directions, bewildered and confused by the many choices available to us. By clinging to Jesus and allowing him to lead us, we will engage all our human faculties in our discipleship and in our evangelizing. As Blessed James Alberione observes: "This devotion is not limited to a simple prayer or some hymns. Rather, it involves the whole person; it gives God complete worship."

Our Secret of Success

Jesus, Divine Teacher, you call us to follow you and to spread the Good News of your Gospel to the ends of the earth. To undertake such a task, we must be holy as our Father is holy.

Yet we are weak, unaware, incapable, and inadequate in so many ways. You, instead, are the Way and the Truth and the Life, the Resurrection, our one and supreme good. We trust in your promise: "I am with you always" (Mt 28:20). We have faith in you alone who assure us, "Whatever you ask the Father in my name, you will receive" (see Jn 14:13).

For our part, we promise to seek only and always your Kingdom, your glory, and peace to all people. We trust that you will give us all we need: grace, discernment, and the means to do good in the world. Multiply our spiritual and apostolic efforts, Lord. We do not doubt you, but we fear our inconstancy and weakness.

Therefore, good Master, through the intercession of Mary, Queen of the Apostles, extend to us the mercy you used with the Apostle Saint Paul, so that, faithfully imitating you here on earth, we may be companions of the saints in heavenly glory.

Based on the prayer Secret of Success
by Blessed James Alberione

God's Dream for Me

Your dream, O Master, is to lay hold of me with
    your divine life.
Your dream is to purify me, to recreate me,
to make me a new person in your image.

Your dream is to fill me with your love, so that I
    love the Father
and all my brothers and sisters just as you do.

Your dream is to draw me to you with the closest
    of bonds,
to unite my heart with yours, to make me strong,
to impart to me your divine power
so that I can overcome evil and be constant in
    doing good.

Your dream is to inflame me with untiring zeal
    to spread your Kingdom.
Your dream is to possess me in this life and in
    the life to come.
May your dream come true! May I be able to
    give all you ask of me. Amen.

Based on the writings of
Blessed James Alberione

"I Am with You"
A Disciple's Dialogue with Jesus Master

I feel alone.	*I am with you.*
I do not understand or see.	*I am your guide.*
I feel unloved.	*I will always love you.*
I feel unimportant.	*I value you always. You are very important to me.*
I feel ignored.	*I hear everything and know everything.*
I feel abused.	*I am your healer and restorer.*
I feel weak.	*I am your strength.*
I feel confused.	*I am your light.*
I feel unwelcome.	*You are always welcome in my presence.*
I feel far away.	*I am always near you.*
I feel unsure	*I am your surety.*
I don't know.	*I know all.*

Be at peace, my child, I am your All in All!

Invocations to Jesus Master

Jesus Master, sanctify my mind and increase my faith.

Jesus, teaching in the Church, draw everyone to yourself.

Jesus Master, deliver me from error, empty thoughts, and spiritual blindness.

Jesus, Way between the Father and us, I offer you everything and await all from you.

Jesus, Way of sanctity, help me to imitate you faithfully.

Jesus Way, grant that I may respond wholeheartedly to the Father's call to holiness.

Jesus Life, live in me, so that I may live in you.

Jesus Life, do not permit anything to separate me from you.

Jesus Life, grant that I may live eternally in the joy of your love.

Jesus Truth, may you shine in the world through me.

Jesus Way, may I faithfully mirror your example for others.

Jesus Life, may I be a channel of your grace and consolation to others.

Based on a prayer of Blessed James Alberione

You in Me

Divine Master, may you be the one who thinks, loves, and speaks—you, not I.

Venerable Mother Thecla Merlo

To Jesus, Our Master and Teacher

Jesus, our Teacher, come and be with us. Be our Life, our true source of joy and happiness. Be our strength and consolation.

Come, Jesus our Master, and be our Way. Help us to realize that the way to heaven can be heaven, because you are the Way. Lead us onward always to our eternal homeland.

Come, Jesus our Master, and be our Truth. Show us the whole truth about ourselves and about you.

Come and help us to leave you free to work in us, to change us. Make us receptive to your will guiding us, your cross in our life, and your fidelity to the Father.

Help us, Lord, to faithfully fulfill our baptismal promises. You are our rock, our saving strength. You are all we have, so in you we place our trust (see Ps 71:3–5).

We recognize you, Jesus, as our true Teacher, our only salvation. Make us more aware of your presence. Draw each person closer to yourself and bring us, your servants, closer to one another, for we come together in your name and because we love you.

May we learn to see you wherever we are and hear your voice wherever we go, that we may contemplate your glory everywhere.

O Jesus Master, burning furnace of love, help us realize how much you love us and every person whom you have redeemed.

Inflame our hearts with that divine fire of love, and then transform our lives so that we may radiate your love to all. Amen.

Lord, You Are My All

Lord, I offer you all out of love. You are my All!

You are with me in times of joy and in times of loss, in times of clarity and in times of confusion, in times of apostolic success and in times of apparent failure. You supply peace, grace, and strength at all moments.

I hope in your promises and offer everything to you in gratitude for your holy will.

Right now I find the work I carry out, both internally and externally, to be hidden in you. Help me to remember that the foundation of a house is hidden from view, yet it sustains the entire building. Strengthen me in virtue and in humility.

Based on a prayer by Venerable Mother Scholastica Rivata

Kenosis[1] in Jesus

Wise Master, you walked with the poor, imparting heavenly wisdom to the secret places of their hearts.

You welcomed people who were ignored and overlooked, the spiritually hungry and thirsty.

You who were rich became poor for our sake, to make us all rich by your poverty (see 2 Cor 8:9).

Our poverty springs from our need of salvation.

We pray for a more just and fraternal society, for solidarity with the poor, for detachment from what keeps us from you and from serving our brothers and sisters.

---

1. From the Greek word meaning "emptiness," in Christian theology *kenosis* refers to the self-emptying of one's will in view of being completely receptive to the divine will.

Prophetic Master, teach us to proclaim the Good News to the poor; that we are all heirs of the Kingdom of God.

You are the radical Teacher who shows us that happiness is the reverse of power, prestige, and possessions.

May your Kingdom come in and through us!

Live in Us, Jesus

O Lord, Jesus Master:
Let your desires be our desires.
Let your thoughts be our thoughts.
Let your actions be our actions.
Let your pain be our pain.
Let your attitudes be our attitudes.
Let your words be our words.
Let your joy be our joy.
Let your prayer be our prayer.
Let us be completely fused to you,
so that it is no longer we who live
but you, O Christ, who live in us and love
    through us. Amen.

Draw Us to You

Jesus, Divine Master, we adore you as the only-begotten Son of God who came to earth to give abundant life to humanity.

We adore you, Word Incarnate, sent by the Father to teach us life-giving truths. You are uncreated Truth. You alone have words of eternal life.

You give us life through Baptism and you nourish us in the Eucharist and in the other sacraments. Live in us, O Jesus, with the outpouring of the Holy Spirit, so that we may love you with our whole mind, strength, and heart, and love our neighbor as ourselves for love of you. Draw us to yourself, so that one day we may possess you eternally in heaven.

Blessed James Alberione

May I Be in You

May I see with your eyes.
May I speak with your tongue.
May I hear with your ears.
May I relish what you relish.
May my hands be yours.
May I pray with your words.

May I treat others as you do.

May I participate in the liturgy as you offered
   yourself: totally.

May I be in you and you in me, to the point that
   I disappear.

May you use my tongue to sing the praises of
   God through the ages.

May you use my heart to love him.

May you use me, in my weaknesses and limitations, to proclaim:

"I am the Good Shepherd; what I desire is mercy."

Blessed James Alberione

Chosen and Loved in Christ Jesus

Lord Jesus, you have loved and chosen us from all
eternity. You marked out for each one of us a journey
toward always vaster horizons, so that we might participate in your gifts of light, grace, and mission.

Thank you, Lord, for revealing to us your mystery
and for having made us worthy, despite our poverty,
to participate in your plan of salvation and to give
you glory. Help us to welcome your word and live it,
transforming it into signs of life and communion for
others.

We beg you, Lord, to renew in us each day your great gift to us, so that we may continue to help build your Kingdom and communicate the divine mystery we have contemplated. Help us to truly work for everyone's happiness (see 2 Cor 1:24).

We Adore You Living in the Church

Jesus, Divine Master, we adore you living in the Church, the Mystical Body of Christ, through which you bring us to eternal life. We thank you for having joined us together as members of the Church, in which you continue to be for humanity the Way, the Truth, and the Life.

We ask that those who do not believe may receive the gift of faith, that those who are separated may be brought into full communion, and that all people may be united in faith, in a common hope, and in charity.

Assist the Church and its leaders; sustain the People of God. Lord Jesus, our wish is yours: that there be one fold under one Shepherd, so that we may all be together in heaven.

Blessed James Alberione

Prayers to Mary,
Queen of the Apostles

In summing up his approach to spirituality, Blessed Alberione wrote: "The Pauline Family strives to live fully the Gospel of Jesus Christ, Way, Truth, and Life, in the spirit of Saint Paul, under the gaze of the Queen of Apostles" (*Abundantes Divitiae Gratiae Suae,* no. 93). The key phrase, "under the gaze" of Mary, indicates that she always watches over us like a loving mother. In turn, we live in Mary's maternal presence. For Alberione, Mary is present in the life of each Christian through every stage, from birth to death. And because presence implies relationship, living in Mary's presence means developing a personal relationship with her.

Alberione's Marian devotion underscores his emphasis on the central place of Jesus Christ in the spiritual life. Just as Mary formed Jesus in her womb, bringing the Word Incarnate into the world, so she forms Jesus in us. Alberione wrote:

> As Mary carried Jesus in her womb from the moment of the angel's words, so she bore the Church in her heart from the moment she heard her Son's words [from the cross]: "Woman, behold your son." She carried the child Jesus in her arms; she carried the newborn Church in her arms. (*Spiritual Exercises*, 1960, p. 514)

Alberione compares this to a new incarnation of Christ: through Mary, we are transformed into Jesus.

Of all Mary's titles, Blessed James Alberione preferred "Queen of the Apostles," though he also called her "our Mother, Teacher, and Queen." Alberione saw Mary as an apostle or evangelizer because she gave Jesus to the world. Because Mary holds this place among the first apostles and the apostles of all times, we hail her as the Mother, Teacher, and Queen of the New Evangelization.

Consenting to the Word

Mary, our Mother, Teacher, and Queen, you gave your consent to the Word and were united completely to the redemptive work of your Son, both in good times and in difficult moments. Teach us to be led by the Spirit as you were, in loving surrender to the Father's will. Teach us to go forward in an obedience that identifies us with Christ, your Son, in his paschal mystery and prepares us to serenely accept adversity. Help us to live the cross in faith and with humility, turning to Christ who loved us and gave himself up for us (see Gal 2:20).

Your fiat, O Mary, is our inspiration, an anchor in difficult times, a light in the darkness. It is a fiat of love and discipleship. Let it echo in our hearts and flow from our lips. Form us in the school of Jesus Master, in total availability to the designs of the heavenly Father.

A Prayer to Say *Yes* Like Mary

O Mary, I place on my lips and in my heart a yes
　　similar to yours:
the *yes* of self-offering; the enthusiastic *yes* of love;
the *yes* of total and generous self-gift;

the serene *yes* of self-surrender to God's will;

the trusting *yes* that is supported by the presence of God;

a *yes* that smiles and is joyful;

a *yes* to what is, what was, what will be;

a *yes* that is offered every day in imitation of your response:

Behold the Lord's servant, let your Word be enfleshed in me (see Lk 1:38).

O Mary, Make Me an Apostle

O Mary, Queen of Apostles, make me an apostle who bears God in my soul and radiates him to those around me. Fill my heart with such an intense love of God that I cannot keep it within myself but must communicate it to others. Make me a vessel capable of bearing Jesus Christ, that he may use me to shed light in the darkness.

O Mother, make me a temple of the Holy Trinity so that all my words, actions, prayers, gestures, and attitudes may speak of the God whom I so love. Make me an apostle, O Mary, like the great Apostle Paul. Amen.

Based on the writings of Blessed James Alberione

Mary, Woman of Communication

O Mother of our Lord Jesus, woman open to the gift of the Spirit, you are the true communicator because you revealed to us the Word of the Father. He sends his Son into the midst of the men and women of every age, so that they might discover his infinite love for them and learn to communicate among themselves as brothers and sisters.

You are the loving Virgin who made herself available to God; the temple of God who silently welcomed and guarded the great mystery of the Word made flesh in your womb, so that our eyes, blinded by sin and by our restless human longings, might contemplate the living Christ and see in him the face of the Father.

You revealed your beloved Son to the poor and the wise in the eloquent poverty of Bethlehem and in the simplicity of the little house in Nazareth. You followed him with total dedication as he carried out his mission, traveling the paths of the world with him up to the moment of his sacrifice on the cross.

In silent adoration, you awaited his glorious resurrection. After his ascension, you remained in prayer with the apostles in the upper room, so as to welcome the Spirit, who helps us understand and communicate, renew the world, and transform our lives in such a way that Christ, your Son, might always live in us.

O Mary, our Lady and Queen of communication, we pray for all who communicate the Gospel. Help us all to transmit a little of your light, your unshakable faith, and your vigilant, hope-filled love. Help us to work in a concrete way to give birth to a new world by working to establish the Kingdom of God.

Receive Me, O Mary

Receive me, Mary, Mother, Teacher, and Queen, among those whom you love, nourish, sanctify, and guide in the school of Jesus Christ, the Divine Master. For those whom God calls, you have special prayers, grace, light, and consolations.

My Master, Jesus Christ, entrusted himself wholly to you from the incarnation to the ascension. I, too, place myself entirely into your hands. Obtain for me the grace to know, imitate, and more deeply love the Divine Master, Way, and Truth, and Life.

Present me to Jesus, for I am an unworthy sinner, and I have no other recommendation to be admitted to his school than your recommendation.

Enlighten my mind, fortify my will, and sanctify my heart, so that I may profit from this great mercy and one day be able to say: "I live now not I, but Christ lives in me" (Gal 2:20).

Blessed James Alberione

Mary, Transformer of the Apostles

Mary, rejoice for the days when you were in the
    upper room
with the apostles and disciples of your Son, Jesus.
You were teacher, comforter, and Mother
to all those gathered in prayer awaiting the
    promised Holy Spirit,
the Spirit with the sevenfold gifts,
Love of the Father and of the Son,
Transformer of the apostles.
Through your prayerful intercession, obtain for us
the grace to realize the value of every human
    person
saved by your Son's fidelity to the Father
to the point of offering his life on the cross.
May the love of Jesus urge us on for the Gospel.
May we carry in our hearts the needs of the
    unborn, of children,

of youth, of adults, of the elderly.
Grant that we may share the message of the
    Gospel
with all people from every continent and culture.
Mary, Mother of the Church and our Mother,
Queen of the Apostles, our intercessor,
    pray for us.

Based on a prayer of Blessed James Alberione

Prayer to Mary for Families

Come, Mary, and dwell in every family,
which we consecrate to you.
May all families receive you with joy.
May they welcome you with the same affection
with which the apostle John brought you into
    his home
after the death of your Son, Jesus.
Obtain for each family member the spiritual
    graces
that they need, just as you brought grace
to Zechariah and Elizabeth's home.
Obtain material graces as well,
just as you obtained the transformation of water
    into wine

for the newlyweds at Cana.

Keep sin far away from every household.

Be for each family light, joy, and sanctification,
as you were in the family of Nazareth.

Obtain for family members an increase in faith,
hope, and love, and a deeper spirit of prayer.

May Jesus, Way, Truth, and Life, dwell in every
home!

Inspire everyone to follow their call,

and may they all be reunited in heaven one day.

Based on a prayer of Blessed James Alberione

Prayer to Mary for a Listening Heart

*"Mary treasured all these words
and pondered them in her heart" (Lk 2:19).*

Mary, when the Angel Gabriel surprised you one day, you listened to his words with an attentive heart. You said "yes" to God's invitation to be the Mother of his Son, and then the Holy Spirit overshadowed you and made you fruitful with divine life. You found joy along with trials in the birth of Jesus, and you treasured everything in your heart.

Intercede for us, that we, too, may have listening hearts: hearts that seek to hear the voice of God in every detail of our lives; hearts ready to respond to the needs of those around us. In the events of each day, whether they are ordinary or remarkable, help us to listen to and understand what God is saying or may be asking of us. Pray that we, like you, may treasure God's word in our hearts and act on it. Amen.

To Our Lady of the Annunciation

May all generations proclaim you blessed, O Mary.

You believed the words the Archangel Gabriel spoke to you, and in you were fulfilled all the great things he had announced to you.

My soul and my entire being praise you, O Mary.

You had faith in the incarnation of God's Son in your virginal womb, and you became the Mother of God.

Then the happiest day in human history dawned. The world was given Jesus, the Son of God, the Divine Teacher and King of the universe.

Faith is a gift of God and the source of everything that is good. O Mary, obtain for us a lively, firm, and active faith—a faith that leads to holiness in this life and the assurance of eternal life in heaven.

May we ponder the words of your beloved Son and hold them in our hearts, just as you contemplated and preserved them in your heart.

May the Gospel be preached to the ends of the earth. May everyone believe the truth of its message so that all people will become, in Jesus Christ, children of God. Amen.

Blessed James Alberione

Queen of Apostles, Pray for Us!

Mary, Queen of Apostles,
pray for us your children
who entrust ourselves entirely to you.
Pray for us so that we may never offend Jesus,
but may love him with all our hearts.
Beneath your mantle, O Mother,
we your children take refuge daily.
Make us all yours.
All that we have is yours.
You are our great teacher.
Teach us, guide us, sustain us,
defend us from every danger
as you have done until now.

And after this our exile
show us Jesus,
the blessed fruit of your womb.

Venerable Mother Thecla Merlo

Praying with Saint Paul

Why should those engaged in the new evangelization be devoted to Saint Paul? There are three very compelling reasons:

1. He is recognized as the greatest evangelizer of all time because of the vast area he covered while preaching the Gospel and because of his ability to inculturate the Good News in these various places;

2. He promptly accepted the Good News when Jesus appeared to him on the road to Damascus, and he molded his entire life to that of Christ; and

3. The Acts of the Apostles, which recounts his journeys of evangelization, and his Letters,

which record what he communicated, are given to us as Sacred Scripture. The Church uses Paul's words and deeds to illustrate the transforming effect of the Christian message on its hearers.

This is why Blessed James Alberione proposed Saint Paul as the model for his foundations. In fact, he claimed that Paul was the real father and founder of the Pauline Family. Alberione challenged all Paulines to strive to be "Paul living today." From Saint Paul they should expect the same concern and encouragement that Paul so generously showered on his own collaborators. Alberione encouraged each Pauline to pray for the knowledge, dedication, and zeal of Saint Paul, so that, by working together, the Gospel might truly reach the ends of the earth.

Saint Paul, Intercede for Us

O holy Apostle, who preached the saving message of Christ and taught men and women how to live in faith, hope, and love, intercede for us that we may imitate your obedience to God's will and may correspond with God's grace working in us.

Grant that we may better know you, love you, and imitate you in your love for Jesus, our Master, and in your dedication to proclaiming the Gospel of salvation; that we may be living members of the Church, the Mystical Body of Jesus Christ; and that all people may know and glorify God.

Lord Jesus, in your mercy grant that, through the powerful intercession of Saint Paul, we may obtain the favor we ask at this time [*mention your petition*]. Amen.

Adapted from a prayer of Blessed James Alberione

My Damascus Events

Light and darkness,
sight and blindness,
power and weakness,
control and surrender.

The "Damascus event" in Paul's life is often
    played out in my own,
though in a less dramatic manner.
Lord Jesus, I meet you in so many ways:
sometimes in silence and prayer
or by stumbling to the ground of my existence.

As I journey through the days of my life,
stop me, call out my name,
send me your dazzling light,
and take hold of me as you took hold of Paul.

Even when I kick against the goad,
even when I lack courage or when fatigue over-
    takes me,
even when I fall again or lose my way—
in all these moments I trust that you are with me
and that your grace is sufficient for me.

Like Paul, let me know how to be companioned
    by others,
allowing myself to be led by those who can point
    out the way to you.
Help me to be willing to listen to what you are
    saying to me through them.
As you sent Paul on mission, I ask that you send
    me forth,

to those persons with whom I am to share your
    Gospel.
Give me, like you gave Paul, the words and
    gestures
that will reveal your mercy to me,
and the love you bear for every person you have
    redeemed.

I Know the One in Whom
I Put My Trust

Saint Paul, you knew the One in whom you put
    your trust….
You handed your life over to Christ.
You are the model of unshakable faith,
of boundless love,
of untiring passion for the Gospel.
God seized you on the road to Damascus
and turned your life upside down.
You followed him to the point of martyrdom
because nothing could separate you from his
    love.
Always straining toward the future,
you traveled the world,

proclaiming to everyone the word that
    enlightens,
heals, comforts, and points out the way.

We ask for even a small portion of your faith.
Open our eyes,
as Christ opened yours,
to help us understand God's love for us.
Help us broach
the inexhaustible horizons of the Word,
which permeated your life through the action of
    the Spirit,
so that we, too, will come to know Christ,
the Lord and end of history;
so that we might come to understand who we are
and place our lives in his hands.

We yearn to contemplate him,
love him, and allow him to live in us—
in our small, personal life stories
as pilgrims here on earth—
so as to learn how to transform our days
and witness to everyone the Lord of our life.
May the entire world come to see
that salvation dwells among us.
May we rediscover the face of Christ
in the poor, in those who suffer, or in those who

seek him without realizing it.
May we open our arms to welcome him in one
    another,
so as to walk together in the light
and rediscover the paths to peace.

Love Never Fails

Saint Paul, you wrote that love bears all things.
Sometimes we don't feel very loving.
You tell us that Jesus preached peace,
yet we aren't always very serene.
How do we live in Christ Jesus
when we are hurting inside?
Hold faith up for us as a shield to quench
the flaming arrows of ambition, envy, self-pity,
    and greed.
Patron of patience, remind us that here we expe-
    rience
light momentary afflictions
compared to the eternal joys that are to come.
Enliven our hope!
You said that light shines out of darkness,
and that Christ shines in our hearts no matter
    what happens.

May we one day be able to say with you
that it is no longer we who live
but Christ who lives in us.
Strengthen our love for him and for our sisters
    and brothers,
especially the most vulnerable.
We ask all of this in the name of Jesus,
and we place all our hope in the living God,
    whose love never fails.

Based on Eph 2:17; Rom 6:11; Eph 6:16–17;
2 Cor 4:6, 17; Gal 2:20; 1 Tim 4:10

Paul's Prayer to Our Triune God

Jesus, encourage us in every affliction so that we may encourage others.

Holy Spirit, come to aid our weakness. We do not know how to express ourselves in prayer as we should, and you intercede for us.

Father, we offer you prayers of gratitude and petition.

Our hope will not be disappointed, because your love has been poured out into our hearts through the Holy Spirit who has been given to us. Amen.

Based on 2 Cor 1:3–4; Rom 8:26; Phil 4:6; Rom 5:5

Teach Us to Live
in Intimacy with Christ

Saint Paul, you lived in deep intimacy with Jesus and spent your life proclaiming him to all God's people. Teach us to do the same.

By virtue of our Baptism, we live in Christ; in him "we live and move and have our being" (Acts 17:28).

We are members of his Body, his dwelling place. Show us what it means to live out of this amazing reality: that, having encountered the love of God in Jesus, we are called to share it as his missionary disciples.

Teach us to carry out the Church's mission in a spirit of praise and thanksgiving, always straining toward the goal: life on high in Christ Jesus.

Recall Saint Paul's Example

Let us be strong. Let us call to mind the examples of strength given us by Saint Paul: in the midst of a thousand difficulties of every type, he continued to travel and preach the Gospel.

Venerable Mother Thecla Merlo

Lead Us, Apostle Paul

Lead us, Paul, in the way of wisdom. Your carefully constructed life came crashing around you when Jesus broke into your intellectual world.

You had it all figured out, just like we do at times. Then came loss, the cross, confusion. Blindness followed, until God enlightened you.

Lead us by the hand, as you were once led, to the waters of our Baptism in Christ. Help us and every person we meet to welcome God's plan and open the door to Christ.

Pray for us, that our words may become words of hope for others. Help us remember that nothing can separate us from Christ's love (see Rom 8:35), and inspire us to give thanks to God at every moment of our lives (see Eph 5:20).

Prayer for Patience

Glorious Saint Paul, from a persecutor of Christianity you became an ardent apostle and evangelizer.

Throughout your life you even suffered imprisonment, scourging, stoning, and shipwreck; you endured persecutions of every kind for the sake of the Gospel.

Your sole desire was to make the Savior, Jesus Christ, known to the farthest bounds of the world, and to that end you shed your blood to the last drop.

Obtain for me the grace to accept the hardships of ill health and the daily struggles of this present life as opportunities to grow in love for Jesus Christ and share in his sufferings.

May the unexpected difficulties that come my way help me to be a more patient, compassionate, and loving person who seeks to assist others in their needs. And, amid the pressures and demands of everyday life, grant me enduring strength to be a faithful and fervent follower of Jesus Christ. Amen.

Blessed James Alberione

Love Builds Up

"'All things are lawful,' but not all things build up"
(1 Cor 10:23).

Lord Jesus Christ, you share equality with God yet you emptied yourself for love of us. Teach us not to seek our own advantage but that of our neighbor.

Help us pursue what leads to peace and builds up others in love. Help us seek to please the other for the good of all. May we never put a stumbling block in the way of another.

Jesus, our Teacher, who taught the way of truth, help us learn to live in harmony with one another, even when we disagree. With one voice may we glorify you and God the Father, in the unity of the Holy Spirit. Amen.

Paul's Prayer for Transformation in Christ

Spirit of God, I ask you for the attitude and mind of Christ. Grant me wisdom and a discerning heart so that I may know what is good, pleasing, and perfect.

Help me to grow in love, and to live my life completely for the Gospel. As I communicate Christ, may I be transformed into Christ.

"For to me, living is Christ and dying is gain!" (Phil 1:21). Amen.

To Know That I Am Loved

Dear Saint Paul,
at your conversion you were astounded
by Jesus's unconditional love for you,
and because of it
you changed the whole direction of your life.
You ultimately poured yourself out
in the service of the Gospel,
to the point of total sacrifice.

Help me to deepen my own awareness
of Jesus' unconditional love for me,
so that I too may have the security and strength
to follow the path of kenosis, of self-emptying
    love,
with and for Jesus.

Prayers for Those Engaged in the New Evangelization

The Church exists to evangelize, having received its missionary mandate directly from the Risen Jesus: "Go therefore and make disciples of all nations. . ." (Mt 28:19). Christ invites each of us, baptized into his Body, to a personal relationship with him that is not meant only for ourselves. As Pope Francis reminds us in the beautiful exhortation *Evangelii Gaudium*, those who have truly encountered Christ and his salvation cannot fail to share with others the love they have received, the joy of the Gospel filling their lives.

But where to begin?

We can learn a lot from Saint Paul, the model of evangelization. His starting point was not activities or projects; it was his great love for Jesus Christ. And this love opened his heart wide to the men and women of his time. Paul became "all things to all people" (1 Cor 9:22), striving to understand their needs in order to bring them to Christ. So must we.

The call to the new evangelization is first a call to love. "Love, love more and more. Love in accordance with the example of Jesus . . . with the heart of Saint Paul," encourages Blessed James Alberione. Such love is a treasure waiting to be shared; there is nothing more precious we can give to others. Alberione reminds us that to evangelize is to be filled with Christ's love to the point of overflowing: "The apostle is a temple of the Most Holy Trinity, within whom God is supremely active. The apostle exudes God from every pore: with words, works, prayers, actions, and attitudes, in public and in private, with one's entire being. Live God! Give God!"

Prayer for Discipleship

Blessed are you, God, the Father of our Lord Jesus Christ, who has blessed us in Christ with every spiritual blessing in the heavens (see Eph 1:3).

Through you, Father, in Christ Jesus we have received grace and our mission as disciples to bring peoples of all nations to faith and obedience in his name (see Rom 1:5).

Make us always ready to proclaim to all the boundless riches of Christ . . . so that the wisdom of God might now be made known through the Church (see Eph 3:8–10).

We beg you, Father, to help us always to lead lives worthy of the vocation to which we are called: in humility, gentleness, and patience, bearing with one another in love, seeking to preserve the unity of the Spirit by the peace that binds us together (see Eph 4:1–3).

Glory to you, Father, whose power working in us can do infinitely more than we can ask or imagine; glory to you from generation to generation in the Church and in Christ Jesus forever and ever (see Eph 3:20–21). Amen.

Living the Gospel

Jesus Master, we feel the challenge to dwell in you, so as to grasp your love for the Father and for all humanity.

We want to respond with hearts just like yours to every person's need for salvation. You are our Eucharistic source of life, our nourishment, and the secret to holiness.

We know that we will find in you, Jesus, a love that urges us to make a gift of ourselves and that prepares us to embrace every new path that may lead to announcing the Gospel.

For the Church's Mission of Evangelization

Bless your Church, Lord, in her task of evangelization. As a pilgrim and evangelizing people, may she be faithful to her mission of proclaiming the salvation you have wrought for everyone.

Help your Church to be an instrument of grace in people's lives; a place of mercy and hope, where all are embraced, loved, forgiven, and strengthened in living the Gospel of Jesus Christ.

Who Will Lead Others to God?

How many people never hear a good word, never hear anything said about God, live as if they did not have an immortal soul. . . . Who will help them? Who will lead them to God?

Venerable Mother Thecla Merlo

Prayer for Apostolic Discernment

Spirit of Wisdom, Communication of the Father and of the Son, open our hearts to hear your voice as we try to discern God's will and the new ways you are opening up for evangelization.

Help us grow in discernment, critical reflection, and apostolic fruitfulness. Make us attentive to the appeals of the Church and of the world in the search for pastoral priorities and programs, in our efforts to share the faith in all its beauty and richness.

May we proclaim Christ in a way that shows others the profound joy that comes from embracing life in him.

We trust that you will inspire us at every turn, and we take courage in your promise: "Proclaim the Good News to all creation; I am with you always."

Jesus, Good Shepherd

Jesus, Good Shepherd,
who brought from heaven the fire of your love,
give us your heart.
Inflame us with desire for the glory of God
and with a great love for our brothers and sisters.
Make us sharers in your mission.
Live in us so that we may radiate you
in word, sacrifice, and pastoral outreach,
in the example of a good life.
Help us as we carry out your pastoral mission in
the Church.
Come, Divine Shepherd, guide us;
may there soon be one flock and one Shepherd.

Blessed James Alberione

The Evangelizer's Power Idea

The power idea that must animate us is the thought of souls. This thought should spur us on. We must be concerned about how we are to reach people and bring them the word of truth and salvation.

Venerable Mother Thecla Merlo

Sent by the Spirit

Lord, you promised to send us the Paraclete, the
  Spirit of truth,
to be with us and to abide within us.
With trust in the strength of this promise, we
  follow your instruction
to go out and bear the fruit of love that will last.
We want to be your witnesses in the world.
Fill us with your love, that we in turn may
share it fully with others.
Holy Spirit, Spouse of the Virgin,
as you descended upon Mary and the apostles
  gathered together in prayer,
be with us, the new apostles of our day.
May our hearts always be open to following
where Christ leads and sends us.
Help us willingly place our personal gifts
at the service of the Church's evangelizing
  mission.
Whatever God may be asking of us—be it
  prayer, work, or suffering—
may we do it wholeheartedly,
aware that we participate in Christ's own saving
  mission.

Prayer to Witness to the Gospel

Jesus, our Master, the Good News you came to bring us has the power to enlighten, to heal, and to save. May I always witness to Gospel values by what I think, say, and do. In whatever ways I can, I want to spread your Good News to as many persons as possible. May everyone come to know you, love you, and follow you, Lord. Amen.

Opening Our Hearts to the World

At times we direct our attention to many small realities and forget the larger ones. We get lost in trifles; we shut ourselves up in our own little world and forget that the real world is a big place and that there are many people out there who are stretching out their hands to us, who are waiting to receive Jesus' light, life, and salvation.

Venerable Mother Thecla Merlo

An Evangelizer's Prayer

Jesus Master, you are the Word, the evangelizer sent by the Father, the Truth that sets us free.

In your goodness, you have called us to participate in the Church's mission of evangelization; to live and share with others the joy of your Gospel.

Live in us, Jesus, with the outpouring of your Holy Spirit.

Help us be attentive to the signs of the times and creative in finding effective ways to share your Good News in all its beauty and goodness.

May everyone welcome and embrace your word, so that the Gospel may transform persons, society, and culture.

Show us how to faithfully respond to our baptismal vocation. Move us beyond our comfort zones, and direct our efforts to fulfill the mission you have entrusted to your Church: *"Go into all the world and proclaim the good news to the whole creation"* (Mk 16:15).

Praying the Beatitudes

Lord, give me poverty of spirit,
so that I always remember that your kingdom is
    my true home.
Comfort me in my sorrows, Lord.
Give me compassion for others who mourn.
Give me a meek heart; empower me to further
    your Kingdom here on earth.
May I hunger and thirst to do your will, Lord;
I trust I will find fulfillment only in you.
Lord, give me a merciful heart,
and surround me with your mercy when I need
    it most and trust in it least.
Purify my heart, Lord, so that I may see your
    presence everywhere, in everyone I meet,
and may I one day see you face to face.
May I bring your peace everywhere I go.
Lord, give me strength, courage, and persever-
    ance when I am persecuted for doing good.
Grant all your children a joyful entrance into the
    kingdom of heaven.

Prayer for Openness of Heart

We beg you, Eternal Wisdom, to give us new vision so as to view persons and events with the eyes of Christ.

Open our hearts to great respect for every human person and for authentic values rooted in the Gospel.

Help us to promote what is true, just, pure, and good, so that all persons may recognize the dignity to which God calls them.

Make us your leaven in the midst of humanity, proclaiming and bringing your salvation into every corner of our world.

Holy Spirit, allow us to be surprised by the "unruly freedom of the word" (*Evangelii Gaudium*, no. 22), which accomplishes its purpose in ways that often exceed our limited perceptions.

Prayer to Incarnate Christ in Our Culture

Jesus, you are the Way, the place where we meet the Father; no one can come to the Father except through you. You are the always new and living Way. To see you is to see the Father.

You are the Truth; to know you is to know the Father, because you are the Word of God. Your truth sets us free. Your Spirit leads us to the whole truth.

You are the Life, given to us by the Father for the life of the world. This life is nourished with your living Bread.

Jesus, Way, Truth, and Life, I want to live in you with my entire being. As I respond to the needs of others, help me incarnate you in the culture and in society.

Based on Jn 14:6, 14:9, 8:32, 16:13, 6:33

May We Be Instruments of Justice and Peace

Father of mercy, you have communicated to us your plan of salvation through your only-begotten Son, Jesus Christ. Today, when so many distractions can lure people away from your love, communicating your Gospel message is a greater challenge than ever. You have called us to a great mission. Although we feel inadequate to fulfill it, we find strength and courage in your Eucharistic presence. May we be instruments of justice, peace, and love in a confused and often violent world that still awaits your Good News.

New Peace Prayer of Saint Francis

Lord Jesus, give us an awareness of the massive
forces threatening our world.

Where there is armed conflict, let us stretch out
our arms to our brothers and sisters.

Where there is abundance, let there be simple
lifestyles and sharing.

Where there is poverty, let there be dignity and
constant striving for justice.

Where there is selfish ambition, let there be
humble service.

Where there is injustice, let there be atonement.

Where there is despair, let there be hope in the
Good News.

Where there are wounds of division, let there be
unity and wholeness.

Help us to be committed to the building of your
kingdom, not seeking to be cared for, but to
care; not expecting to be served, but to serve
others; not desiring material security, but
placing our security in your love.

For it is only in loving imitation of you, Lord,
that we can discover the healing springs of
life to bring about new birth on our earth and
hope for the world. Amen.

The World Is Waiting

The entire world is our mission field. We must love all people in order to do good to all.

Venerable Mother Thecla Merlo

Prayer for Evangelization

Lord God, set our hearts ablaze with a desire to live our faith fully and to share it freely with others.

In our efforts to proclaim the Gospel, help us to be joyful, credible witnesses to Christ.

Only with him can we transform ourselves and the world we live in.

Open our hearts to recognize the spiritual and material needs of our brothers and sisters, to hear the cries of the poor, and to be deeply moved by the plight of all who suffer.

Show us the path to wisdom—through a response inspired by love, humble and generous service, and compassion toward all.

May everyone experience the joy that comes from encountering Jesus.

For Those Who Do Not Know God

Lord, have mercy on those who do not know you, who do not love you! Inspire many people with the desire to make you known and loved!

Venerable Mother Thecla Merlo

Creed of Those Called to Evangelize

We believe that God chose us in him before the world began, to be holy and blameless in his sight.

We believe that those whom he foreknew he predestined to share the image of his Son.

We believe that God, who had set us apart before we were born and called us by his favor, chose to reveal his Son in us, that we might spread among all people the good tidings concerning him.

We believe that God has saved us and called us to a holy life, not because of any merit of ours, but according to his own design—the grace held out to us in Christ Jesus before the world began.

We believe that we are apostles by vocation, servants of Christ Jesus, set apart to announce the Gospel of God.

We believe God chose the weak of this world to shame the strong, so that our faith would not rest on the wisdom of men but on the power of God.

We believe that to each one God has given the manifestation of the Spirit for the common good.

We believe that we must live a life worthy of the calling we have received, with perfect humility, meekness, and patience, seeking to grow in all things toward him.

We believe that all things work together for the good of those who love God, who have been called according to his decree.

We believe in him whose power now at work in us can do immeasurably more than we ask or imagine.

We believe that he who has begun the good work in us will carry it through to completion, right up to the day of Christ Jesus, because he who calls us is faithful.

Based on Eph 1:4; Rom 8:29; Gal 1:15–16; 2 Tim 1:9; Rom 1:1; 1 Cor 1:27; 1 Cor 2:5; 1 Cor 12:7; Eph 4:1–2; Rom 8:28; Eph 3:20; Phil 1:6; 1 Thes 5:24

Evangelization Prayer for One Who Is Elderly or Infirm

Divine Master, because of illness I am not physically able to do as much as I could before. I offer you these later years of my life. Accept my love, prayers, and sufferings in reparation for my sins and for the sins of humanity. Grant salvation to all people on the face of the earth. Help me continue to witness to your love through a joy-filled life offered in service of the Gospel. Allow me the grace to move through each remaining day with calmness and kindness. I offer everything, even my death, for your glory and the good of all, and I trust in your love to lead me home. Amen.

A Catechist's Prayer

Jesus our Master, send your Spirit to empower me to teach your truth, walk in your way, and live by your life. May those to whom I minister see you in me, and through you the Father. Guide and guard them, even in life's darkest hours, for you have redeemed them by your blood. In your mercy lead all of us into the everlasting joy of Father, Son, and Holy Spirit. Amen.

A Youth Minister's Prayer

Lord Jesus, lover of young people, give me your love for youth. Help me find ways to reach the minds and hearts of the young people I minister to, so that they will develop a relationship with you built on and supported by faith. As they mature, may they choose what is good, what will help them flourish in your love and lead them to true happiness. Holy Spirit, inspire me to understand the world of young people so that I may evangelize from within their culture. Enkindle in youth the desire to bear your light to one another and to live the Beatitudes in an exciting journey of true discipleship. Amen.

To Radiate God

May we be apostles who carry God in our souls and radiate God around ourselves. May we be saints, with hearts on fire with love for God and for our brothers and sisters. Lord, we ask that you make this fire so great that we cannot but speak of all we have seen and touched in you. May we, like Saint Paul, invite others to quench their thirst in you. May you, Father, Son, and Spirit, be active in us, seen in us, felt through our words and deeds, touched through our kindness, known through our gestures and attitudes, and revealed through our entire being. Amen.

How Beautiful to Communicate Jesus

Let us see to it that our hearts are filled with God so as to bring him to souls. How beautiful and holy it is to communicate Jesus to others—that Jesus whom we want to always carry in the center of our hearts. When our hearts are filled with the love of God, then this love necessarily overflows onto the world.

Venerable Mother Thecla Merlo

Prayer to Be Trustworthy Companions

Like the disciples journeying to Emmaus, may we who are engaged in the work of the new evangelization feel the presence of Jesus burning in our hearts. May we be trustworthy companions who lead others to him through our sharing and proclamation of the word.

May the fire of Jesus, enkindled in us by God's Spirit, lead others to become disciples, formed in the image of Christ our Savior.

Evangelizing in a Communications Culture

As human beings we are constantly communicating. We live in a world permeated by all types of communication. There are devices available to keep us in touch with friends and open us up to messages from around the globe. New media inventions enhance and develop the new digital continent at an unprecedented rate.

The rapid development of communications media has changed the face of our world. With the new media, information is more and more accessible to more and more people. We can expand our knowledge and build up new relationships, stay connected with people halfway around the globe, unite in prayer for urgent intentions, take immediate action to respond to urgent needs—such as natural disasters, grow in solidarity, discover connections previously unimagined, and reach out to others in an unprecedented way with the joy of the Gospel.

The amazing array of technology does, however, give rise to some concerns. Social media in particular reshape our daily communication. We ask ourselves how we can avoid being *too connected* technologically, how to counteract the temptation of allowing text messaging to replace our dinner conversation with loved ones, how to sort through the overabundance of information and entertainment to focus on what is essential, ignoring the distraction of consumerism and tantalizing media messages that lead to superficiality, fragmentation, and isolation. And how can we prevent the spread of error and manipulation of others when individuals and groups with bad intentions misuse the media?

These are legitimate concerns. Living in our media world requires prayer, discernment in our media choices, thoughtfulness about the media messages we are exposed to, and constantly striving toward balance. The media are gifts of God and offer marvelous potential for evangelization. But they also pose temptations for thoughtless or improper use.

And when media are wrongly used to create pornography or the depiction of wanton violence, they are deformative, influencing people toward sin and a disregard for the dignity of others.

In the Pauline tradition and in the Church today, we are urgently called to use the media for good and to make use of their potential to preach the Good News. We praise God for these gifts of human ingenuity. We ask the wisdom to make of them instruments of new evangelization. We also dedicate our efforts and prayers for the conversion of those who misuse these means and for those led astray by improper messages.

Prayer is the ultimate human communication, so in our prayer we ask God to help us to evangelize the culture of communication in which we are privileged to live.

A Eucharistic Offertory for the Media
(Pauline Offertory)

Father, in union with all those celebrating the Eucharist throughout the world, I wish to unite myself with the heart and intentions of your beloved Son, Jesus, who offered his life for our salvation:

— that the media may always be used to support the good of each person and the common good; to uplift the sacred dignity of every human person, especially those who are poor and most vulnerable; to nurture marriage and family life; to bring about solidarity, peace, greater justice, and equality for all people; and to build respect for the gifts of God's creation;

— in reparation for the errors and scandals spread throughout the world through the misuse of the media;

— to call down your mercy upon those who have been deceived or manipulated by the misuse of the media, and led away from your fatherly love;

— for the conversion of those who have spread error, violence, or a disregard for the dignity of the person by wrongly using the media and rejecting the teaching of Christ and his Church;

— that we may follow Christ alone whom you, Father, in your boundless love, sent into the world, saying, "This is my beloved Son, hear him";

— to acknowledge and to make known that Jesus alone, the Word Incarnate, is the perfect Teacher, the trustworthy Way who leads to knowledge of you, Father, and to a participation in your very life;

— that in the Church the number of priests, religious, and lay people who are dedicated as apostles of the media will increase in number and grow in holiness, making resound throughout the world the message of salvation;

— that all those who work in the media with good will (writers, artists, directors, editors, technicians, producers, advertisers, and distributors) may grow in wisdom and uprightness, living and spreading worthy human and Christian values;

— that the undertakings of Catholics in all forms of media may continually increase, so that by more effectively promoting genuine human and Christian values, they will silence the voices that spread error and evil;

— that well aware of our inadequacy and unworthiness, we may recognize our need to draw near the font of life with great humility and trust and be nourished with your Word, Father, and with the Body of Christ, invoking light, love, and mercy for all men and women.

Based on a prayer of Blessed James Alberione

Prayer for Using the Media in the New Evangelization

O God, to communicate your love to all, you sent your only Son, Jesus Christ, into the world and made him our Master and Shepherd, the Way, Truth, and Life of humanity.

Grant that all means of communication—print, film, radio, television, the Internet, and all new media—may be used for your glory and the good of all people.

Inspire everyone of good will to assist with prayer, action, and financial support, so that through these powerful means the Church may preach the Gospel to all peoples. Amen.

Blessed James Alberione

Canticle of Praise for the Media

May you be praised, Lord God, for the printed word—bread for our minds, light for our lives.

We give thanks for the talents and dedication of all who serve the truth in love, and for all whose technical and professional skills make possible the production of books, newspapers, magazines, and reviews.

We celebrate, Lord, the modern marvel of television, which brings into the heart of our homes the joy and pain of human living. Music, drama, and laughter are shared in ways undreamed of in the past.

May you be praised, Lord God, for the radio, which soars on the wings of the wind and provides for each nation an immediate channel for news, views, and entertainment, and a means of offering to the listening world its own distinctive voice.

We celebrate, Lord, the writers, artists, directors, and all those whose gifts light both theater and cinema and provide audiences with a heightened awareness of their human condition.

We celebrate the wonder of digital communication, which manifests a new iconography and links people around the globe in solidarity of faith, hope, and love.

We thank you, Lord God, for the unending Pentecost of your creative Holy Spirit, which enables your sons and daughters to be afire with your truth, beauty, and goodness.

May the blind see, the deaf hear, and the poor receive justice through the proclamation of the Good News via today's media.

Together let us rejoice in the God-given talents and the creative gifts of those who promote the dignity of the human person, and who build communion among peoples the world over through their dedication and love.

Based on the writings of Blessed James Alberione

Prayer to Saint Paul for the Media: A New Place of Evangelization

Saint Paul, traveler for the Gospel, proclaimer of the Good News, you asked your fellow Christians to pray "that the word of the Lord may spread rapidly and be glorified" (2 Thes 3:1).

Today God's word travels most swiftly through the media. Living in the era of global communication, we use these marvelous means not only for information and entertainment, but also as a way of connecting with others.

We recognize their potential for all that is good and beautiful, as well as for the opposite.

Saint Paul, pray for those creative persons who produce all forms of media and for those who use their productions.

May the men and women who shape media messages, and those who receive those messages, promote human dignity and foster respectful communication. In this way, both the message and the medium will be channels for what is good, true, and beautiful.

Pray also for those who, like you, seek to proclaim God's word in this new place of evangelization.

Through the sometimes blaring and relentless voices of the media, may we be attuned to God's voice coming through these means: that tiny, whispering sound, which is often the way God speaks to us. And when we hear the soft voice of God's word, may we be filled with grace and peace from God our Father and Jesus Christ our Lord.

"Whatever is true, whatever is honorable, whatever is just, whatever is pure, whatever is pleasing, whatever is commendable, if there is any excellence and if there is anything worthy of praise, think about these things" (Phil 4:8).

Prayer for True Communication

Jesus, our Way, by washing the feet of your disciples you provided a meaningful expression of your love for them. This gesture challenges us to look into our own lives and evaluate our love in light of yours. To be a true communicator, we need to empty ourselves in order to be filled with love for our brothers and sisters. Lead us to always more selfless giving. May we realize that we will discover your face precisely in true communication and service to others.

A Communicator's Prayer

Lord, make me an instrument of your grace.
Where there is ignorance, let me bring inspiration;
Where there is prejudice, understanding;
Where there is weariness, strength;
Where there is ugliness, beauty;
Where there is loneliness, companionship;
Where there is sadness, joy;

Where there is fear, courage;
Where there is doubt, faith;
Where there is hatred, love.
Lord, fill my mind with your truth,
> my heart with your love, my whole being
> with your Spirit.
Grant me the supreme gift of forgetfulness of
> self in service of others, and make your mis-
> sion mine.

Prayer for Creativity
in the Work of Evangelizing

Lord Jesus, our Divine Master, you call us to communicate your mystery of salvation. This call spurs us on to reach out to a world undergoing continual rapid and unexpected changes. It compels us to practice discernment, to be creative in new evangelization projects, and to evaluate them in light of your word.

Transform us into your announcement; for with the deepest yearnings of our heart we desire to bring you to the people of our time.

We are fully aware that we are poor, small, and insufficient in everything, but we trust in you.

Help us to become true bearers of your word, to live in an attitude of ongoing conversion, and to look to the future with hope.

By means of our words, actions, or work, our writing, art, or performance, our dance, production, and our very lives, may we witness to the truth that you are the center of our life and of all lives.

O Lord, help us to make our communication with you and among our families, friends, and neighbors a starting point for building a world of genuine union that will be transformed into full communion with you.

To Jesus, Master of Images

Jesus, Divine Master and Shepherd, you used the common, well-known image of shepherd and sheep to describe your relationship with your people, with each of us. The image of the Good Shepherd was so effective that it shocked some people in your audience. But you know the value and power of image, story, and proverb, and you frequently used these to communicate the freshness of your message. Give us hearts like your own: shepherds' hearts that hear the cries of their flock. Help us to fully support and embrace human life, and to touch your flesh in others. May we be so imbued with your love that our proclamation never becomes old or routine. Give us creativity and courage to speak in the language of our time and to discover new ways to penetrate society with the Gospel.

Help Us Be Discerning Users of the Media

Spirit of Wisdom, teach us to discern the messages that come from the media.

Assist us with your grace, O Divine Spirit! Help us to use these means to discern the signs of the times, to search for a Christian response, to derive motives for prayer. We ask this through the perfect Communicator, Jesus Christ our Lord. Amen.

A Photographer's Prayer

O Lord, help me to communicate the beauty of your image in all creation: in people, nature, events. Grant that this photographic medium may proclaim the thousand silent words of your glory, greatness, goodness, and love. May it go beyond a picture of external realities to capture your delicacy, your wisdom, your unique beauty. Allow it to portray the expressions of the human heart that cannot be verbalized, so as to create a bond of understanding, unity, and solidarity among all God's children. May it awaken us to your hidden presence, spur us to action, deepen our contemplation of your unfathomable riches, and encourage each soul to draw nearer to you in confidence, from earthly shadows to eternal light.

A Graphic Designer's Prayer

God, Creator of the universe, you put in perfect order what had been chaos at the beginning of time. In justice and right the plans of your great design took on form.

With the touch that only a Master Artist can give, you took the elements of nature and fashioned the most marvelous work of art the world will ever know. Words fall short to describe the timeless beauty of your creation, which never ceases to delight and inspire. From the invisible atom to the human person, your presence is found throughout the universe, sustaining everything in being.

In Jesus Christ, our Divine Master, you expressed the fullness of your infinite beauty and goodness. In him you revealed yourself; through him you have revealed us to ourselves.

In his light we artists are to shed light upon the path and destiny of humanity in every age (see Pope John Paul II's *Letter to Artists*, no. 14). For this we offer and give you the world of art and design. Consecrate them for your purposes. Take all our creative energies—our tools, projects, time, and resources. Attentive to the aesthetic quality that our works demand, may each visual we produce be a reflection of your splendor shining on the face of Christ (see 2 Cor 4:6).

An Artist's Prayer

Heavenly Father, we bless you for the gift of beauty, color, and sound that can raise our hearts from the struggles and pains of this earth and remind us of the glories of our homeland to come.

Awaken the artist that lies deep within the souls of each of us, so we can rediscover ourselves in meaningful creative activity. Remind us that art is the sacred imitation of you, our loving Creator. Give success to the work of our hands, O Lord.

We ask this for the glory of your name.

Proclaiming Christ
through the Media Arts

Lord of all our hopes, you are the Living One who conquered death and sent your Spirit to renew all things. You guide the way of all men and women who journey through history, and you sustain the commitment of all those who participate in the creative work of renewing the universe.

We offer you, Lord, the joys and successes of all your children committed to the various fields of social communications.

We present their constant search for you so that they may proclaim you in truth, justice, freedom, and love. Lord, guide those who use the various media arts to open new horizons of hope, of true life, of solidarity, of communication, and of communion.

With hope we look forward to a new world, which you call us to build through our work as evangelizers.

We pray that our efforts may contribute to building a world of peace and unity. God of salvation, love, and hope, enfold all who search for you in your most tender embrace.

A Musician's Prayer

Father, Son, and Holy Spirit, thank you for the gift of music. Thank you for giving us song, so that we can proclaim your word in a way that is fitting, beautiful, and delightful.

Thank you for giving me a musical talent to share with your Church and for allowing me to contribute to the liturgy through my song.

Conform my mind and heart to the inspired words I will sing. May those who witness my delight in song know that you are the true source of beauty and joy in life.

Jesus Master, may all those who respond to the beauty of this music be taken up into my prayer. Together, may we be strengthened in hope, in faith, and in a spirit of praise of the one God, supremely true and beautiful, the one and highest good.

In the presence of the angels I will sing your praise (see Ps 138). Amen.

Make Me Life for the World

Knead me, Lord Jesus, into the world of communication, as eucharistic bread that will nourish others.

Teach me the new media languages that will give your message the best paths to reach minds and hearts.

Guide me as I send words into cyberspace; inspire my choice of activity in social media.

Your word is alive and active, like yeast in the dough of our world.

Thank you for calling me to participate in your plan of peace.

May my communication be modeled on you, Jesus, who entered our world and took on a body.

You communicated through words, attitudes, gestures, silence, symbols, and movements.

You shared your life experiences, and in your great love offered yourself to the point of giving your life for us.

Glory to you, Blessed Trinity, Communicator par excellence!

Communication expressed among you, Father, Son, and Spirit, is total self-offering. May my communication be the fruit of love.

Prayer for Good Use of the Media

We praise you, Jesus Master, for having enlightened the human mind to discover the audio, visual, electronic, and digital media: film, radio, television, the Internet, social media, and other new technologies. They are new paths for mission and for the education and uplifting of society.

You created everything for us, as we are for Christ. May these inventions, too, sing your glory as Creator and Savior.

Lead us not into temptation, Lord, but deliver us from the danger of misusing the gifts you have given us with such wisdom and love.

Lead those responsible for these media to work with charity and respect for human dignity. May they always sow the seed of good wheat and keep watch so that the enemy may never sow weeds. Enlighten all listeners, viewers, and media users to seek the fonts of living water.

To atone for those who misuse these media, we offer you our daily evangelizing efforts in union with all the holy Masses celebrated today throughout the world. We promise always to use media in a way that will help us grow in holiness and for the spread of the Gospel.

Jesus Master, through the intercession of Mary, Queen of Apostles, and of Saint Paul the Apostle, grant that through these media the world may come to know you as the Way, and Truth, and Life of humanity.

Based on a prayer of Blessed James Alberione

To Saint Gabriel the Archangel, Patron of the Electronic and Digital Media

Father in heaven, we thank you for having chosen Saint Gabriel from among the angels to bring the message of the incarnation and the redemption of humanity. Mary accepted the tidings with faith, and your Son became incarnate. By dying on the cross and rising from the dead, he redeemed all people.

But the majority of people still have not received the message of salvation.

Saint Gabriel, patron of films, radio, television, and all social and digital media, implore Jesus Master that the Church may use these powerful means to preach the divine truth to be believed, the way to be followed.

May these gifts of God unite all peoples and help them cooperate with God's plan of salvation.

May they never be used to harm anyone or undermine God's loving design.

May everyone receive and accept the message of Jesus Christ.

Saint Gabriel, pray for us and for the apostolate of film, radio, television, and all social media. Amen.

Based on a prayer of Blessed James Alberione

A Prayer Before Writing

O Jesus, Divine Master, I offer you my pen and keyboard for the intentions with which you preached your Gospel. May every word be only and always for the glory of God and peace to all people. May everyone know you, O Jesus Truth! May everyone wholeheartedly follow you, O Jesus Way! May all hearts love you, O Jesus Life!

Give me clarity of thought, pure intentions, and grace in writing. May my words reiterate your word; may Saint Paul the writer guide me; may every piece of writing I produce be modeled on the Bible.

O Mary, Mother, Teacher, and Queen, who gave to the world the Divine Word Incarnate, look down lovingly upon me and bless this apostolate that I shall carry out with you and for you.

Based on a prayer of Blessed James Alberione

A Storyteller's Prayer

Loving Creator God, you have made me in your image and have given me a share in your own creative power. You have given me the awesome call to listen deeply and to gently hold and nurture the fragile breath of inspiration.

Allow a new understanding of truth and beauty to come into being in me. Work in me as I decisively shape and mold intuition into words and stories.

Teach me how to nurture this gift of creativity, and to believe that you want to work through me. Slow me down so that I can listen attentively. I trust that you will inspire me, guide me, lead me.

Jesus, Master Storyteller, you who are the very Incarnation of the Father's being, help me to image the mystery of God and of the human person in what I write. You used the power of image, story, and proverb to communicate the freshness of your message. May my storytelling—whether spoken, written, or visual—open the human soul to the sense of the eternal. Let everything I write celebrate the wonder and sacredness of human life, uplifting those who will hear, read, or see what I write.

Holy Spirit, illumine me from within; give me new vision; fill my heart with your freedom and my decisions with your energy.

Stir up my creative intuition and give me the courage to write honestly and deeply, past all fear.

Make of me a prophet, speaking your truth with freshness and relevance. May everything I write contain a glimmer of your beauty.

Make of my stories and, above all, the story of my life, masterpieces that reflect your glory. Amen.

Praying the News

Lord, I check the news every day, and every day
I am shocked and saddened, but also inspired
    and encouraged.

Your Sacred Scripture says:
"What has been is what will be,
and what has been done is what will be done;
there is nothing new under the sun" (Eccl 1:9).

We share the same joys and sorrows
that men and women have experienced through-
    out the ages.
But what takes place today around me and
throughout your world is news.
Each incident, each event *is* something new
because it is happening now to someone today.
This *now* is part of the time you redeemed,
and each *someone* is your beloved child destined
    for eternal life.

As I take in the news today, dear Lord,
inspire me to pray for those involved in the
    stories,
those affected by the events,
and all who announce and receive the news.
Give me the gift of awareness
and a sense of responsibility,
especially toward the most vulnerable in our
    society and in our world.
Expand my heart, Lord, and give me a share of
    your love,
that I may embrace all that is news today. Amen.

The Word of God

Blessed James Alberione dreamed of "imbuing all human thought and knowledge with the Gospel." He spoke of the Bible as *the* book for all humanity. He desired to proclaim the word of God everywhere, using all the modern means of communication.

The Bible is an encounter with the living Word of God, Jesus Christ. In Pauline houses the Bible is enthroned in chapels and other areas to remind us that we are to become a living word, to witness Christ in an authentic way. This is what will make us effective evangelizers, as Pope Francis reminds us: "The Lord wants to make use of us as living, free, and creative beings who let his word enter their own hearts before then passing it on to others" (*Evangelii Gaudium*, no. 151).

Pauline spirituality draws deeply from two well-springs: the word of God and the Eucharist.

Speak Through Us, Lord

Gracious God, you spoke the Word, and all
    things came to be in you.
Resounding Word, silence the many voices that
    surround us and become our sole Voice.
Let your new incarnation penetrate all parts of
    the world through sound waves.
O Word, you commission us to speak, to reach
    your people with the message of salvation,
    healing, peace.
Come, speak through us.
Allow us to give voice to the joy of your message.
Come, your world stands before you in silent,
    hopeful expectation.

At Home with the Word

Lord God, as Saint Paul poured out his heart to
the world through his letters, may his writings find a
home in me.

Send your Holy Spirit to guide me in the great
adventure of reading and studying Paul's writings.

May I savor the depth of truth contained in them,
growing in knowledge and in the freedom of the
children of God.

As I read Paul's words, may I understand the difficult passages; be moved, inspired, and comforted; and be conformed to the image of Christ.

Living according to the word, may I then better share its riches with others. Amen.

A Heart Open to Your Word

Jesus, give us a heart open to your word.

Send your Spirit to remind us of the truths you teach, the witness of your life, and the wisdom of your way.

Thank you for the gift of Sacred Scripture, your living word and food for our journey.

May we preserve your words in our mind and meditate on them in our heart as your Mother Mary did, so that all our words and actions may proclaim you.

Treasures of Your Word

Jesus, true light, you enlighten everyone who comes into the world.

I know you have come from God to be our Teacher, and that you teach us God's ways in truth.

The words you have spoken to us are spirit and life, but who is worthy to break the seals and open the book (see Rev 5)?

You alone are worthy—the lamb who was slain for us. You have redeemed us, not by silver or gold, but by your precious blood!

Grant that I may learn your unfathomable riches and the mysteries of the kingdom. Show me the treasures of the wisdom and knowledge of God that are hidden in your word (see Col 2:3).

Grant that it may penetrate my soul, enlighten my steps, and brighten my way—until the day dawns when darkness vanishes forever. Amen.

Blessed James Alberione

Before Reading Sacred Scripture

I welcome you, O Divine Word, with an attentive, docile, and prayerful heart.

Open my mind and my heart to hear your voice and to understand and do your will.

Grant that I may be evangelized by the all-sur-passing knowledge of Christ. Teach me wisdom. Be the light that illumines, purifies, prunes, and heals, so that Christ Truth may be formed in me.

Transform me, Word of the Father, so that I may grow in union with you and as an apostle of your word.

Live in me and in our home, church, workplace, and community, so that together we can grow in faith and discern events around us in order to respond to the Spirit's invitations.

Your word is light—it is Way, Truth, and Life. Amen.

After Reading Sacred Scripture

Jesus, our Savior,
you appeared on earth to teach us,
so that, rejecting self-sufficiency and worldly
    desires,
we might live lives that are sober, just, and
    reverent (see Titus 2:11–12).
Grant that your word may change us within,
so we may become like you,
who through mercy and love
made yourself like us. Amen.

Blessed James Alberione

Prayer of an Apostle of the Word

Your word is our light and strength, Lord.

Help us to welcome it with open and listening hearts.

Like Mary, we want to give our consent to the word

through our daily adherence to your divine plan for us.

May we be built up by listening to your word

and sharing it with one another, so that it may transform us.

Allow us to be evangelized by the all-surpassing knowledge of Christ.

We bring to you the hopes, joys, and anxieties of the world, to intercede for all and to discern the ways that the Spirit is opening up for the word.

Make of us servants who communicate the mystery of Christ to all peoples.

Father, with Mary, who welcomed, treasured, and lived the word,

we unite ourselves to the mission of Jesus, your Son,

in total availability to your designs.

To Be Your Living Word

Jesus Master, you are the Word who touches and
moves, heals and makes holy.
Enter and fully captivate my mind and imagina-
tion.
Tame and transform every energy, passion, and
desire, so that I truly may be all yours.
Then, in communion with your Body, the
Church, make of me a living word for our
world—to communicate the beauty of your
love through my every word and action.

Becoming Bread Broken for the World

Heavenly Father, we desire to enter fully into the
mystery of your covenant with your people, in the life
and mission of the Church.

Grant us the grace to advance toward the fullness
of charity, so that we may seek only your glory and
peace to all people.

Thus we can truly become a sign of your Risen
Christ in the world.

Grant us the grace to welcome your word and
allow its message to find a home in us.

May our communion with Jesus in the Eucharist and in the word always be our light and strength. We offer ourselves with him to you, Father.

May we, too, become bread broken for the life of many. Amen.

Jesus, Word of the Father

Jesus, Word of the Father, we thank you for the many examples of profound communication you have given us in the Gospel.

May we understand the yearnings of people today, and seek to touch their lives by pointing the way to union with you.

Set our hearts on fire so we may communicate your love to all. Help us to respect the persons with whom we communicate, in a spirit of understanding and compassion.

Jesus, divine communicator, help us to radiate you in our lives and to proclaim you with all the means at our disposal—whether in person, through social media, or with hidden and humble gestures. Do not let us overlook anything that we can use to communicate your love.

Prayer to Mary
for the Ministers of the Word

O Mary,
you who gave birth
to the Word made flesh,
be present among us.
Assist, inspire, and comfort
the ministers of the word.

O Mary,
you who are Queen of the Apostles,
intercede with your protection,
that the light of the Gospel
may reach all peoples.
May heaven be filled with those
who sing the hymn of glory to the Most Holy
    Trinity. Amen.

Blessed James Alberione

The Holy Eucharist

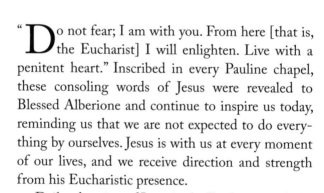

"Do not fear; I am with you. From here [that is, the Eucharist] I will enlighten. Live with a penitent heart." Inscribed in every Pauline chapel, these consoling words of Jesus were revealed to Blessed Alberione and continue to inspire us today, reminding us that we are not expected to do everything by ourselves. Jesus is with us at every moment of our lives, and we receive direction and strength from his Eucharistic presence.

Daily adoration of Jesus in the Eucharist is a hallmark of Pauline prayer. It centers our life in Christ. It is the privileged moment in which we renew our personal encounter with his saving love, impelling us to share this gift with others.

In speaking of Eucharistic adoration, Blessed Alberione cautioned, "Avoid formalism." He spoke instead of Eucharistic adoration as a visit with Jesus as with a friend, which does not begin and end in chapel, but permeates all our hours, occupations, and relationships. It deepens our relationship with him and forms in us a spirit of continual prayer, in which Jesus enlightens us about everything. More and more we are able to allow Jesus to become alive and active in us. Then gradually, as Alberione explained, "Life is transformed into prayer, and prayer gives life." And this life is the reason we evangelize; it is the treasure we offer to others.

A Visit with Jesus

This Eucharistic visit is the meeting of my soul
and my entire being with you, Jesus.
I am here, the creature before the Creator,
the disciple before the Divine Master.
I need healing in your presence, Doctor of souls.
I am poor, appealing to you, the rich one;
I come thirsty to drink at your font.
I am here before you with my limitations and
    failings.
In times of temptation, I seek you as my sure
    refuge.
As a blind person, I search for your light.
I am a friend visiting with you, my truest friend.
As a lost sheep I seek you, Divine Shepherd.
My heart has gone astray and I find you, Jesus
    Way.
I am a fool seeking wisdom, Jesus Truth.
In you I find my life's meaning, Jesus Life.
In you I find my All.

Based on the writings of Blessed James Alberione

Prayer to Begin
Eucharistic Adoration

I believe, my God, that I am in your presence,
that you are looking at me
and listening to my prayer.
You are so great and so holy; I adore you.
You have given me all; I thank you.
I have often offended you, and I ask your pardon
    with all my heart.
You are so merciful; I ask of you all the graces
that you know I need.

Dwell in My Heart, Lord

Lord, feed me with your Body and with your word, and I will be able to run along your paths.

Lord, make me understand your mysteries of salvation, and I will see your glory on the face of the other. I hunger and thirst for the Bread of Life and for the word. Satiate my spirit and quench my thirst.

Teach me to ponder your word, to listen to the groanings of the Spirit who dwells in my heart.

Help me to discover the roots of your love, the sprouts of hope, and the fruits of justice and peace that flourish in the bosom of our world, announcing a new springtime.

Come, Holy Spirit, come fill my heart.

To Jesus, Our Eucharistic Master

Jesus, our Eucharistic Master, you feed us with your abundant teaching. You are the Bread of wisdom and revelation; you nourish all who come to you in faith. Fill our empty hearts with your life-giving word.

Strengthened at the table of your divine wisdom, may we break and share the bread of your word with others.

O Jesus Christ, you are the Eucharistic source of eternal life. You feed us with your Flesh and Blood at the sacramental banquet of your heavenly and glorified Body.

Nourished by your sacred Body and Blood, and united with your paschal sacrifice, let us be transformed into Eucharistic bread, broken and shared for all.

O loving Lord, you are the Eucharist and the Divine Master. You are the Living Bread come down from heaven.

We love you; we believe in you; we want to be nourished by you now and at the eternal banquet. Amen.

Act of Trust in the Promises of Jesus

Jesus, we believe you are the Word who became flesh and lived among us, offering us grace and truth.

Jesus, we believe you are the Lamb of God who takes away our sins.

Jesus, we believe you are the Master who invites us to discipleship, growth, and ever greater love.

Jesus, we believe you are God's beloved Son, sent into the world to save us.

Jesus, we believe you are Living Water, who quenches our thirst for meaning with love, peace, and truth, offering us abundant life!

Jesus, we believe you are the Bread of Life, broken and given for the life of the world.

Jesus, we believe you are the Light of the world, who frees us from darkness and answers the deepest questions of our hearts.

Jesus, we believe you are the Good Shepherd who laid down his life for us, who keeps us safe and calls us to shepherd others.

Jesus, we believe you are the Resurrection, promising eternal life to all who believe in you.

Jesus, we believe you are the Master who became the servant of all and who invites us to imitate your loving service.

Jesus, we believe you are the living and true Vine, who promises plentiful life and sends us forth to bear fruit.

Jesus, we believe you are the Way, the Truth, and the Life of the world, inviting us to be transformed in you so that we can witness your love and saving mercy to others.

The Eucharist: Bread of the Strong

Loving Father, you are compassionate and provident. You are our loving and living God.

In your Son, Jesus Christ, the Living Bread that came down from heaven, is found the strength that restores and leads us to eternal life.

Strengthened by this food, help us to be compassionate to the poor and needy.

By our preferential care for the weakest among us, let them savor the spiritual riches that come from you. May we always live in the love of our Lord Jesus Christ.

Let the Holy Spirit animate us always. Together with you may we serve as bread of the strong for our disheartened brothers and sisters.

We love you; we serve you; we give you glory and praise, now and forever. Amen.

The Eucharist: Bread of the Covenant

Loving Father, we thank you for the gift of the Eucharist, which is the bread of unity, the bread of spiritual renewal, and the bread of wisdom.

It is also the bread that gives us the grace to live out the New Covenant sealed in the blood of Christ.

By the light of your word and by nourishing us at the altar-table of the Eucharistic Body and Blood of your Son, Jesus Christ, may we be true to our destiny as your covenant people.

We also pray for married couples, that their love-covenant may draw strength from Christ's unconditional love for the Bride-Church.

Today, we renew our covenant with you in the sacrament of the Eucharist, and in the Mass we unite in participation at the altar of the world.

We love and praise you, for you are compassionate and faithful, now and forever. Amen.

May My Life Be a Liturgy

O mystery of the Father's incomprehensible love for his children, made known in Jesus through the gift of the Spirit! I contemplate the total gift of yourself to us.

I ask that I may respond with a total gift of self through full participation in the Eucharistic liturgy.

Participating in your mystery, may I be a living communication of your love to my sisters and brothers. May my life become a liturgy offering glory to you and peace to all men and women.

Emmaus Prayer

Lord, after your death on the cross the disciples walking toward Emmaus were filled with fear and confusion.

You, Jesus, Teacher and Shepherd, met them on the way. In your compassion you walked with them and taught them. When you spoke, their hearts burned within them. "Stay with us," they entreated.

You went in with them, and when you sat at table you took the bread and blessed and broke it, and gave it to them. Then their eyes were opened and they recognized you (see Lk 24:13ff.).

Stay with us, Jesus. May we always gaze on you, Good Shepherd, so that we may come to know you. You are God's compassion for his people. In you his merciful love takes on a human face.

You ask us, "Why are you frightened?" and then you reassure us, "Look at my hands and my feet. . . . Touch me and see" (Lk 24:39).

Through your incarnation you allow us to touch God, to receive God in the Eucharist, to cling to God in our fears, and to hear the reassuring words: Do not fear; I am with you.

"Do not let your hearts be troubled, and do not let them be afraid" (Jn 14:27).

Prayer of the Disciple of the Eucharistic Master

Father in heaven, may we learn to welcome the gift of the Holy Spirit, so that we may become a living sacrifice that is holy and pleasing to you.

Make us living and active members of the Church, as we follow your Son, our Eucharistic Master.

Grant that being rooted and hidden in him, and conformed to his image, we may praise and adore you, make reparation and implore grace for the Church and the whole world.

May the ministers of the Gospel be holy.

May all people welcome your word in accordance with the spirit of the Church.

May they be nourished by the Bread of Life and drink their fill at the font of salvation.

We ask all this through Christ, our Lord.

Based on a prayer by Blessed Timothy Giaccardo

My Beloved Jesus

I believe that you are present before me in the tabernacle. Although I cannot see you or touch you, I believe that you are here with me.

You are happy that I have come to visit, and you desire to share the riches of Trinitarian life with me during this sacred time in my day.

Jesus, please help me to focus on you during this time. Help me to let go of all the worries in my mind, all that distracts me from hearing what you have to say. Do not let the precious pearls of your wisdom fall on deaf ears.

I am weak and only able to pray effectively when you give me the grace to do so. Please help me today, because I so desire to spend time with you, to refresh my spirit.

I desire to renew my faith, hope, and love so that I can be a better representative of you in the world. Help me to listen, to gather all the wisdom you have for me this day so that I may become holier, not wasting even one minute that could bring me closer to you.

Dear Jesus, although my prayer will not be perfect today, please accept it for all the intentions of the world, for my own holiness, and for the intentions of the Holy Father.

I love you and trust in you, Jesus.

Bread of Wisdom

Loving Father,
we yearn for wisdom and long for the gift of
    eternal life.
In Jesus Christ, your Son,
you feed us with the bread of wisdom and com-
    passion.
In the Eucharistic meal,
we partake of his Flesh, which is true food,
and drink of his Blood, which is true drink.
By the paschal mystery of Christ's passion,
    death, and resurrection,

you have revealed your infinite wisdom
and enable us to delight in your love and life
    eternal.
Help us to serve you faithfully, O Father,
following the example of Jesus,
through the power of the Holy Spirit.
We thank you and bless you,
now and forever. Amen.

Prayers of Reconciliation and Forgiveness

Blessed James Alberione wrote: "The process of sanctification is a process of 'Christification': 'until Christ is formed in you' (Gal 4:19). We will be saints in the measure in which we live the life of Jesus Christ—or better, in the measure in which Jesus Christ lives in us. The Christian is another Christ. This is what Saint Paul says of himself: 'It is no longer I who live, but it is Christ who lives in me' (Gal 2:20). Christification comes about gradually until we reach 'the measure of the full stature of Christ' (Eph 4:13), just as a child gradually grows into an adult."

Alberione encouraged his followers to make a daily examination of conscience—a review of one's life in light of the Gospel—as an essential means of growing in Christian holiness. In the examination of conscience we prayerfully look over our day to thank God for the graces we have received, to determine whether we have sinned or not, and to see how we are concretely progressing in virtue. The period of examination concludes with asking God's forgiveness for personal failings and renewing our resolutions to live a more virtuous life by means of God's grace.

Another helpful means to spiritual growth is the Ignatian method of examination, called the Consciousness Examen, which involves becoming conscious or aware of God's presence and action in our daily lives. The examen leads us to revisit particular moments when we felt God's presence, and it encourages personal discernment of what God may be saying to us or showing us. It is most effective when practiced regularly, as a standard part of one's daily schedule.

The examen can be prayed simply, following these five steps:

1. We remind ourselves that we are in the presence of God and ask for a deeper awareness of this mystery of the divine indwelling.

2. We spend some time thanking God for all the graces and favors we have received. This is an important step, for it makes us more aware of God's graciousness toward us.

3. We then ask the Holy Spirit to enlighten us as we examine our life. The Spirit helps us to see into our hearts and discern the areas where he is calling us to be more open to grace.

4. We review the day, paying attention to the times that stand out more, such as occasions that prompted strong feelings and emotions. We look into our heart, examining our motives in acting and how we responded to various persons.

5. Finally, we bring all of this to God in prayer, asking for insight and expressing sorrow for whatever ways we have failed to live in love. Thinking of how we might act differently in the future, we ask God for the help we need to grow in virtue and love.

The practice of opening ourselves wholly to the purifying light and transforming power of God, the Master of our lives, enables him to gradually conform us to Christ through the action of his Spirit. This, Blessed James Alberione reminds us, is the goal of every Christian. We stand in daily need of God's grace and mercy—a posture that allows us again and again to encounter the Lord's personal, saving love. And this renewed experience of salvation impels us to share unreservedly the love that has changed our lives forever.

Prayer Before
an Examination of Conscience

I place myself in your presence, Blessed Trinity.

As I reflect on this day, my limitations come to mind, as well as the amazing strength you gave me through your gifts of faith, hope, and love.

My humanity reveals itself through choices that I made involving my thoughts, words, actions, and in what I did not do. I want to do what is good, but I do not always do it. I do not want to do what is wrong, but I often do it anyway (see Rom 7:19).

I give you thanks for the wonders of your grace reflected in those moments that I did carry out your will.

Help me clothe myself with your compassion, kindness, humility, gentleness, and patience (see Col 3:12).

Prayer After
an Examination of Conscience

Thank you, Jesus Master, my Good Shepherd. Trusting in your divine mercy, I begin again. I ask for forgiveness, even as I forgive others. I forgive as you have forgiven me.

I praise and thank you for the sacrament of Confession, where I meet your mercy and love. I ask for courage to begin anew, right now, remembering that your love never fails because your Spirit of life sets me free from the law of sin and death.

Help me to put on love, which binds all virtues in harmony. Let your peace reign in my heart. Amen.

May I See Myself as You See Me

Holy Spirit, I come before you with trust
   in your love.
Fill me with your light and grace
so that I may see myself as you see me.
Guide me back to your path when I stray.
Help me to follow your inspirations
so that I may always do your will,
for that is the path to peace. Amen.

To Jesus, the Divine Healer

May you be blessed, Divine Master,
because you made yourself similar to us
in order to make us similar to God.

You repaired the ruin
caused by sin and disorder.
You showed us
that we can inherit divine happiness
if we live a life similar to yours.
Grant that we may know you, imitate you, and
love you.

Blessed James Alberione

For Unfailing Hope

Lord Jesus, you see my entire life: past, present, and future. You know my thoughts and feelings. You see how hard life can be, how unfair it can seem at times. In all the confusion, one thing is certain: your love for me never changes. I place all my hope in you.

You embrace me as I am. You walk with me and guide me. Help me to recognize your presence and to follow where you lead with trust. You desire only the greatest good for me; you are on my side. I place all my hope in you.

Help me to know how much you want to be part of my life. Widen the limits of my heart to make room for you and through you for others. You are God, my Savior. I place all my hope in you.

May the God of hope fill us with all joy and peace in believing, so that we might abound in hope by the power of the Holy Spirit (see Rom 15:13).

Prayer to Grow in Love

Jesus Master, fill my heart with a love . . .

that is patient, not troubled over the imperfections I notice in others;

that is charitable and loving, and that seeks to do good for others;

that is not jealous, but rejoices when others succeed in doing better than I;

that is not careless, but is attentive, vigilant, and discerning;

that is not proud, but acts with simplicity and sincerity, out of consideration for others;

that is not ambitious, intolerant, or difficult to satisfy;

that is not selfish, but seeks the interests of God and of my neighbor for the sake of God;

that does not react in anger, but is humble and gentle;

that never thinks evil or is distrustful;

that neither makes hasty judgments nor rejects others;

that rejoices in the truth, happy to see others
    esteemed;
that bears all things, surrendering to whatever
    God permits;
that believes and hopes in everything—especially
    in the good that exists within others.
Love never ends.

Venerable Mother Thecla Merlo
(Based on 1 Corinthians 13)

To Live and Communicate Peace

Lord Jesus, Prince of peace, we see our chaotic world today with its anguish and fear.

We feel ourselves vulnerable because we, too, are prisoners of the uncertainties and difficulties of our history.

We raise our hands to you, in this darkest of nights, and entrust all humanity to you.

We are threatened by the storms of war, but we want to remain unshaken in the certainty that a new day will come; because you, Lord, are always at work, even when all is cold and dark around us.

Help us to think of peace, to hope in peace, to live as persons of peace, and to build peace around us; to promote a hospitable and welcoming culture, and justice for the entire world.

Be with all those throughout the world who suffer persecution for your name.

Give them courage in their adversities and strength to persevere in faith.

Enable us to nurture reconciliation and forgiveness, so that peace may penetrate our thoughts and feelings, making us credible signs of understanding and communion.

Lord, you conquered violence and death that we may live.

Help us become living icons of your love, so that peace may truly be the *home for all*.

Spiritual Healing Prayer

Holy Spirit, through the intercession of the Queen of Pentecost, heal my mind of ignorance, forgetfulness, obstinacy, prejudice, error, and lack of reflection. Form Wisdom, Jesus Christ Truth, in my mind.

Heal my heart of apathy, mistrust, bad inclinations, disordered passions, and unhealthy attachments. Form good taste, feelings, and inclinations —Jesus Christ Life, in my heart.

Heal my will of fickleness, inconstancy, sloth, stubbornness, bad habits, and lack of will power. Form Jesus Christ Way in my will—renewed love for whatever Jesus Christ loves and for Jesus Christ himself.

Fill me with your gifts, O Spirit, infusing intelligence with the gift of understanding, insight with the gift of heavenly wisdom, comprehension with the gift of divine knowledge, good sense with the gift of counsel, justice with the gift of piety, strength with the gift of spiritual fortitude, temperance with the gift of fear of the Lord.

Based on a prayer by Blessed James Alberione

Wonders of Mercy

Your mercy is infinite; I will never be able to
    fully understand it.
I want to adore rather than examine your
    mercy.
How is it that you chose me, a small creature,
    a great sinner?
I am a miracle of God!
Your call of the twelve apostles transformed them;
your call to me has made me a new person.

I am immersed in Christ: his interests are my
   interests; his teaching, my teaching.
My life is that of Christ.
I carry out his actions, or better, he carries them
   out in me.

Based on the writings of Blessed James Alberione

List of Contributors

In addition to prayers drawn from *The Prayers of the Pauline Family* (for private use), the prayers in this book were composed by (alphabetical by last name):

Alberione, Blessed James, SSP
Founder of the Pauline Family (1884–1971)

Alves, Mary Emmanuel, FSP

Anderson, Karen Marie, FSP

Brown, Laura Rhoderica, FSP

Burns, Helena Raphael, FSP

Carrara, Giovannamaria, FSP

Cesarato, Maria Regina, PDDM

Curley, Marie Paul, FSP

Heady, Susan James, FSP

Heffernan, Anne Eileen, FSP

Hill, Mary Lea, FSP

Hirsch, Ancilla Christine, FSP

Flanagan, Anne Joan, FSP

Giaccardo, Blessed Timothy, SSP
*First priest and Vicar General of the Society
of Saint Paul (1896–1948)*

Gitonga, Jacqueline Jean-Marie, FSP

Jablonski, Patricia Edward, FSP

Kerry, Margaret, FSP

Lane, Helen Rita, FSP

McGowan, Laura Rosemarie, FSP

Merlo, Venerable Mother Thecla, FSP
*Co-Foundress of the Daughters of Saint Paul
(1894–1964)*

Moran, Margaret Edward, FSP

Moss, Mary Martha, FSP

Noble, Theresa Aletheia, FSP

Quaglini, M. Agnes, FSP

Richards, Virginia Helen, FSP

Rivera, Venerable Mother Scholastica, PDDM
*First Mother General of the Sister Disciples
of the Divine Master (1897–1987)*

Santos, Germana, FSP

Tapang, Mary Margaret, PDDM

Tessa, Mary Caroline, FSP

Trouvé, Marianne Lorraine, FSP

Wallace, Susan Helen, FSP

Wilson, Mary Leonora, FSP

Zanatta, Majorina, FSP

*Other prayers from various Pauline prayer guides
by Daughters of Saint Paul, whose contributions remain
anonymous, have been compiled in this book.*

BOOKS & MEDIA

The Daughters of St. Paul operate book and media centers at the following addresses. Visit, call, or write the one nearest you today, or find us at www.pauline.org

CALIFORNIA

3908 Sepulveda Blvd, Culver City, CA 90230	310-397-8676
935 Brewster Avenue, Redwood City, CA 94063	650-369-4230
5945 Balboa Avenue, San Diego, CA 92111	858-565-9181

FLORIDA

145 S.W. 107th Avenue, Miami, FL 33174	305-559-6715

HAWAII

1143 Bishop Street, Honolulu, HI 96813	808-521-2731

ILLINOIS

172 North Michigan Avenue, Chicago, IL 60601	312-346-4228

LOUISIANA

4403 Veterans Memorial Blvd, Metairie, LA 70006	504-887-7631

MASSACHUSETTS

885 Providence Hwy, Dedham, MA 02026	781-326-5385

MISSOURI

9804 Watson Road, St. Louis, MO 63126	314-965-3512

NEW YORK

64 W. 38th Street, New York, NY 10018	212-754-1110

SOUTH CAROLINA

243 King Street, Charleston, SC 29401	843-577-0175

TEXAS

Currently no book center; for parish exhibits or outreach evangelization, contact: 210-569-0500 or SanAntonio@paulinemedia.com

VIRGINIA

1025 King Street, Alexandria, VA 22314	703-549-3806

CANADA

3022 Dufferin Street, Toronto, ON M6B 3T5	416-781-9131